Guru Nanak's
JAPUJI
A Look Anew

Satnam Kaur
S.K. Saxena

DK
PRINTWORLD
Publishers of Indian Traditions

Cataloging in Publication Data — DK
[Courtesy: D.K. Agencies (P) Ltd. <docinfo@dkagencies.com>]

Satnam Kaur.
Guru Nanak's Japuji : a look anew / Satnam Kaur, S.K. Saxena.
p. cm.
Includes text of Japuji in Panjabi (Gurmukhi, Devanagari and roman).
Includes bibliographical references (p.).
ISBN: 9788124607015

1. Nānak, Guru, 1469-1538. Japuji. 2. Sikhism – Prayers and devotions. I. Saxena, S. K. II. Nānak, Guru, 1469-1538. Japuji. III. Title.

DDC 294.682 23

ISBN 13: 978-81-246-0701-5
First published in India in 2013

Printed and published by:
D.K. Printworld (P) Ltd.
Regd. Office : *'Vedaśrī,'* F-395, Sudarshan Park
(Metro Station: Ramesh Nagar)
New Delhi – 110 015.
Phones : (011) 2545 3975, 2546 6019; *Fax* : 2546 5926
e-mail : indology@dkprintworld.com
Web : www.dkprintworld.com

Guru Nanak's

JAPUJI

A Look Anew

To the memory of

Sardar Gurbaksh Singh Bakshi

Preface

GURU Nanak's *Japuji* is a great work. Our abilities, contrarily, are quite limited. Yet we cannot stop hoping that this little book will do some good to every thoughtful reader.

The one clear aim of *Japuji* is to show us the way to get rid of suffering. This is borne out by the Guru's crowning emphasis:

gāviai suṇiai mani rakhīai bhāu ।
dukhu parhari sukhu ghari lai jāi ॥[1]

Now, in so far as we all pine for riddance from suffering when it strikes us, *Japuji*'s relevance to the whole of humanity is incontestable. No one, however, can gain anything from the work if it is read cursorily, as our holy books of religion often are. We too, in our present attempt, have not been able to do justice to all that *Japuji* says – and suggests. Some of its esoteric details had to be passed over because they appeared to be wholly beyond us. On the other hand, we have been able to clarify, we hope, quite a few[2] such subtle points punctuating the text as could not be ignored; and, what is more, to put such cognate details together as occur distantly in the text. What has kept us

---

1 *Sri Guru Granth Sahib*, Standard 1430 pages, Amritsar: Bhai Jawahar Singh Kirpal Singh and Co.; *Japuji, pauḍī* 5.

2 But, surely *not every* subtle point.

glued to the work, in spite of the heavy demands it makes on both understanding and imagination, is not merely the richness and profundity of Guru Nanak's words, but the catholicity of spirit for which he is well known. He does not go with any specific theological creed, but prefers to emphasize instead what is much more basic and of far greater overall value, that is, genuine self-control and collateral inner purity:

āī panthī sagal jamātī mani jītai jagu jītu ||[3]

In our own imperfect way, we have all along tried to be clear and consistent in our writing; and this should be of help to all those who wish to make the most of this cardinal work of Guru Nanak.

It is precisely this hope that we regard as the one immediate reward of our labours. The close of this preface however has to be, first, a word of gratitude to those whose *translations* of this holy work, *Japuji* – specially the widely known ones done by S. Manmohan Singh, S. Gurbachan Singh Talib and Dr. Gopal Singh – have been of great help to us all along; and, second, some helpful hints for the reader. In respect of the relevant *commentaries*, we may add, our choice could not but be restricted. We wanted one by an author who has been widely respected not only for his knowledge of our rich and diverse religious traditions, but just as well for his personal devoutness and catholicity of interest in religious matters. This, we thought, was essential not only for balancing, *in our writing*, the demands of reason with the evidence of personal religious experience and insights, but for keeping true to the very wide relevance of

---

3 *Japuji*: *pauḍī* 28.

Guru Nanak's thought. So we fell back on Vinoba Bhave's small but invaluable work, *Japuji* (Sarva Seva Sangh Prakashan, Rajghat, Varanasi).[4] Vinoba Bhave is not only *consistently* – yet nowhere without reason – *very sympathetic* to the essential import of Guru Nanak's entire writing, but is able to draw our attention to quite a few subtleties in Guru's literary craftsmanship. One of these is the use of some such words from different languages as have a kindred, yet not identical meaning, so adroitly that the little semantic difference does nothing to ruffle understanding. Above all, Vinoba Bhave cites apt parallels of so many insightful utterances of the Guru *from traditional wisdom of our saints, representing different regions of the country and multiple paradigms of devout living*, that *Japuji* finally comes to appear what it truly is – i.e. not just a single, isolated work, but a quintessential index of quite a few values and emphases of our timeless ethico-religious culture.

We cannot, however, close this preface before adding the following for readers' assistance:

(a) The original text of *Japuji*, in three different languages – namely, Gurmukhi, Devanāgarī and English (as Romanized) – has been provided at the close of the book.

---

[4] In this context it is heartening to note that, revealing an open-mindedness which is intrinsic to their faith, some eminent Sikh scholars like S. Gurbanchan Singh Talib have spoken very highly of Vinoba's work on *Japuji*. See here the following: "Few, indeed, could be better equipped to undertake such a task as Vinobaji has done here". Gurbachan Singh Talib's translation of Vinoba Bhave's commentary on *Japuji*, Patiala: Publication Bureau, Punjabi University, 1989, p. ix.

(b) Guide to transliteration follows the "table of contents".

(c) In respect of spellings we have all along followed the orthographic pattern of *Gurbānī* itself. It may, however, be noted that in reading its text, short vowels are to be quietly passed over, instead of being clearly articulated.

The reader is now welcome to turn to Chapter I: Introductory. If, as we hope, he finds the book not only sensible but good to *look at*, the credit has to go to Mr. Vinay Jain who has designed the cover not only beautifully, but with due care for the character of the book's content, and to our unfailing publisher, Mr. Susheel K. Mittal, who never tires of removing stray errors in printing. Typing the manuscript has been the responsibility of Mr. A.N. Sharma and Mrs. Manjit Kaur Matta.

18 Januray 2013

Satnam Kaur
S.K. Saxena

Contents

Transliteration Chart

Hindi	Gurmukhi	Roman	Hindi	Gurmukhi	Roman
अ	ਅ	a	ठ	ਠ	ṭh
आ (ा)	ਆ (ਾ)	ā	ड/ड़	ਡ	ḍ/ṛ
इ (ि)	ਇ (ਿ)	i	ढ/ढ़	ਢ	ḍh/ṛh
ई (ी)	ਈ (ੀ)	ī	ण	ਣ	ṇ
उ (ु)	ਉ (ੁ)	u	त	ਤ	t
ऊ (ू)	ਊ (ੂ)	ū	थ	ਥ	th
ऋ (ृ)		r̥	द	ਦ	d
ॠ (ॄ)		r̥̄	ध	ਧ	dh
ए (े)	ਏ (ੇ)	e	न	ਨ	n
ऐ (ै)	ਐ (ੈ)	ai	प	ਪ	p
ओ (ो)	ਓ (ੋ)	o	फ	ਫ	ph
औ (ौ)	ਔ (ੌ)	au	ब	ਬ	b
अं (ं)	ਅੰ (ੰ)	ṁ	भ	ਭ	bh
अः (ः)		ḥ	म	ਮ	m
क	ਕ	k	य	ਯ	y
ख	ਖ	kh	र	ਰ	r
ग	ਗ	g	ल	ਲ	l
घ	ਘ	gh	व	ਵ	v
ङ	ਙ	ṅ	श		ś
च	ਚ	ch	ष	ਸ਼	ṣ
छ	ਛ	chh	स	ਸ	s
ज	ਜ	j	ह	ਹ	h
झ	ਝ	jh	क्ष		kṣ
ञ	ਞ	ñ	त्र		tr
ट	ਟ	ṭ	ज्ञ		gy/jña

1

Introductory

It is not easy to see how a single, incidental remark by an intensely devout person can serve as impulse to attempt an original interpretation of a spiritual classic. Yet this has exactly been the genesis of this little book on Guru Nanak's *Japuji*. In his brief but scholarly – yet insightful – commentary on this great work, Vinoba Bhave aptly remarks that the more deeply we reflect on this primal work of the Guru, the more rewarding will be our search for its essential, even esoteric significance.[1] It is indeed with this sane counsel in mind that we now venture to turn to the *mūl mantra* which provides a kind of sacrosanct preface to *Japuji*.

It goes without saying that the spiritual sensitivity which lends a manifest loftiness to the *mantra* is inaccessible to us. All that we can do is to try to interpret what its words appear to signify, in a way which has to be not merely clear and self-consistent, but all along open to whatever – in the work's total compass – may appear relevant to the point at issue.

We may agree that, as the Guru himself declares, no amount of mere thinking, howsoever detailed and deep it be, can be quite true to what is commonly regarded as the

---

1 Vinoba Bhave, *Japuji*, Raj Ghat, Varanasi: Sarva Seva Sangh Prakashan, p. 31.

ultimate (spiritual) reality – say, God or *Brahman*.[2] In fact, we ourselves hope to show a little later – i.e. where we seek to *interpret* God's creativity in a way which appeared quite plausible to us – that one has ultimately to forego the merely theoretical approach in favour of the personal testimony of spiritually competent persons (*āpta vākya*). At the same time, however, if we do not try our best to comprehend what this basic work of Guru Nanak, that is *Japuji*, has to say, how shall we come by, and get imbued with his teaching, and act in accordance with it, as he surely wants us to – for *our own* ultimate felicity?[3]

What is more, in so far as *Japuji* provides just the quintessence, not the whole of Guru Nanak's ethico-religious views, for the sake of adequacy we will also have to refer to some such relevant material as is outside the pale of *Japuji*, though this primal work will of course remain the focus of our attention all along.

We are aware that *Japuji* has been regarded by quite a few eminent scholars as a great, creative – even poetic[4] –

---

2 *sochai sochi na hovaī je sochī lakh vār* (*pauḍī* 1 of *Japuji*); *Sri Guru Granth Sahib*, English and Punjabi translation, vol. I, Amritsar: Shiromani Gurdwara Parbandhak Committee (tr. Manmohan Singh), 7th edn., 2004, p. 1.

3 A closer – i.e. a little more thoughtful – look at *Japuji* is demanded also by such laments of some eminent scholars as the following: "The world is poorer for its ignorance of the Sikh Scriptures". – W.H. Mcleod

4 "Guru Nanak is an extraordinarily complex *poet* who writes simply; he skilfully holds together strains of intricate and elusive thought". – Kartar Singh Duggal (comp. and tr.), *The Japuji, Sikh Morning Prayer*, Delhi: UBS Publishers and Distributors, 2000, p. 15

work *in itself*. We see no reason to disagree. Yet, as we set out to *interpret* it, its *context* cannot be ignored. Its author is no less a person than Guru Nanak, *and* it is meant to show us the Way supreme. So we have to bear in mind, all along: (a) the edifying tenor of the Guru's own life, on the one hand; and (b) his gracious insistence on *our* moral uplift, on the other. Hopefully, all our interpretative effort that follows will be determined by this fullness of concern.

Here, incidentally, we think it necessary to distinguish this rather uncommon venture from *translations* of *Japuji*, of which there has been quite an impressive output from learned scholars. A translation has to go strictly by the order of the text it has to deal with. It is neither free nor is expected to integrate (for better understanding) the content of different parts of the book being translated, howsoever cognate this content may appear to be. Nor is it a part of the translator's function to visualize the context, human or merely situational, in which the work in question might have shaped itself. We, on the other hand, are not at all so constrained. Our work, as interpreters, requires us to heed all along the dual context we have just alluded to. In fact, we have found it gainful to do so. This should become clear as we proceed.

What is more, we have also found it needful to heed even the *order* of Guru's prolific utterances, be they eulogistic, didactic or gently persuasive. Why does he insist, one may ask, so emphatically on God's eternality (*ādi sachu . . . hosī bhī sachu*) almost immediately after the *mūl mantra*? Our answer here is: he *had* to do it, to counter our likely diffidence in accepting the reality of a *kartāpurakhu* who is possessed of such celestial attributes as are very likely to make us gape in wonder and disbelief. The emphasis in question is, in fact, demanded by our very finiteness, and concomitant inability to comprehend what appears to be utterly unearthly. Be it noted here that, however ebullient the Guru's utterances may seem to be, they are always significant, vehicles (at times) of some profound meaning or experience, and duly warranted by the running context.

What is more, because these *utterances* are naturally located at different places in the text, the reader too will have to take care to integrate such of them as are in fact related in Guru's overall view of the subject. Thus, the following line:

dukhu parhari sukhu ghari lai jāi ।
–*pauḍī* 5

has to be taken not only along with the immediately preceding ones:

nānak gāvīai . . . mani rakhīai bhāu ॥

(all occurring in the fifth *pauḍī*), but with the following lines that distinguish the very first *pauḍī*:

kiv sachiārā hoiye kiv kūḍai tuṭai pāli ॥

because these words allude to the essential linkage between the genesis of authentic faith and truth. Similarly, where the Guru prays fervently as follows:

so mai visari na jāi,

the full (if partly implicit) basis of the prayerful yearning is provided not merely by the immediately preceding words:

sabhnā jīā kā iku dātā,

but, we suggest, by the Guru's ingrained remembrance of the following:

sāchā sāhibu sāchu nāi bhākhiā bhāu apāru ।
– *pauḍī* 4

Clearly, the Guru's devotedness to God's other attributes cannot be taken to disappear when he makes just one of them – say, "the Giver of all life" – his anchor in prayer. They all enliven him through and through. Otherwise, how can one account for the fervour with which the whole of *Japuji* scintillates?[5]

---

[5] The point becomes clear when we compare the writing here with that of Gandhiji who too was unquestionably a man of God.

2

The Mūl Mantra

THIS profound *mantra* may be said to set the tone for all that follows. Here, in a moment of *revelatory incandescence* maybe, the Guru does not merely vouch for the oneness of God, but quickly enumerates some of His attributes which are transcendent,[1] by and large. We hasten to add that our use of the two italicized words (following the opening sentence) in the present context is by no means merely rhetorical. It is justified by Vinoba Bhave's authentic remark that *mantra*s, of which the *Mūl Mantra* we are dealing with may be taken as a typical instance, are not created or written by anyone, but are just revealed to *r̥ṣi*s (men of consummate spiritual sensitivity).[2] Now, such a revelation cannot be a cool perception of the everyday kind. It is bound to make the devotee's being vibrate with spiritual fervour. In enunciating the *Mūl Mantra* the Guru too seems to be overwhelmed by a direct feel of the majesty of God, and is therefore impelled to blazon His superlative attributes straightaway. Why this is followed presently by a categorical affirmation of God's absolute perpetuity has already been explained. The Guru just wants to assure us that, howsoever otherworldly *He* may appear to be, God *is* unquestionably there, *has been* there

---

1 That is, beyond normal human experience.

2 Vinoba Bhave, *Japuji*, p. 33.

all along, and will continue to be *ad infinitum*[3] – an assurance (we may add) that should serve as ballast to our commitment to *Nāmajapa*.[4]

Now, apart from His eternity which Guru Nanak affirms categorically, and which has to be accepted as the evidence of his consummate openness to spiritual truths – i.e. as *śabda pramāṇa* – the other attributes of God listed in the *Mūl Mantra*, which are all alike significant, call for some explicit attention. But before we turn to interpret them – not only individually, but in relation to each other – two questions may be posed and addressed in respect of the *mantra* as a whole:

(a) Why does it open and run as it does?

(b) Why is it titled as it is, i.e. as *Mūl Mantra*?

Now, as we turn to these questions, one particular thought dominates our minds. As the Guru sets out to compose *Japuji*, his being is already ripe with a lifetime of intense devoutness; and therefore he is ready and equipped to receive intimations of the highest spiritual significance. Like every other important text which provides quintessential religious insights, this *mantra* too (as Vinoba Bhave suggests) is revealed to the Guru. He opens to it reverently; acknowledges its source, the peerless One, by chanting *Ek Oṁkār* and affirming that He alone is true

---

3 *ādi sachu jugādi sachu* ।
hai bhī sachu nānak hosī bhī sachu ॥

We hasten to add that, as we shall see a little later, this ontological insistence has helped us in interpreting the word *Satināmu* better than it is commonly done.

4 See, here, the following: *jiu bhāvi tiu nām japāī* – *Sri Guru Granth Sahib*, p. 154.

(*Satināmu*), the basic reality, partly because of the fact (we may say) that God alone has been his own anchor throughout his life; and then sets out forthwith to list (some of) His transcendent or ethereal attributes, as they have been revealed to him – say, as an expression of His grace (*Gurprasādī*).[5] God and His attributes are both basic (or *mūl*) and unique in significance. This is our answer to the two questions (a, b) we set out to deal with.

Such creative interpreting, we may add, is not only possible in respect of, but is warranted by quite a few emphases in the text of *Japuji* itself; and, what is more, a little recourse to it may well be expected to quell some likely scepticism. Take, for instance, the following categorical utterance:

> *hukmai andari sabhu ko bāhari hukm na koi* ||[6]

Now, even a cursory look at these lines can evoke an uneasy question. If this is really so – i.e. if God controls all that is there – *are we* neither free nor expected to do anything on our own? At this point, we suggest, we have to take note of the Guru's own following emphatic utterance, though it comes well after the words just cited:

> *sāchā sāhibu sāchu nāi bhākhiā bhāu apāru* |
> *ākhahi mangahi dehi dehi dāti kare dātāru* ||[7]

If, as these lofty and heartening words declare, God's

---

5 Our view at this point gains added support from the way we have tried to outline the Guru's own attitude to God, a little later.

6 *Japuji, pauḍī* 2.

7 Ibid., *pauḍī* 4.

language – i.e. *His* very way of dealing with (or governing) the world (of both man and nature) – is uninhibited love (*bhāu apāru*), His *hukam*, whatever it be in respect of its details, cannot but be thoroughly beneficient on the whole, though *we* may not be able to see this total truth. What, then, is the sense in pressing for our *own* freedom in (or against) *His hukam*? Further, in so far as, if given the choice, we would all prefer consummate felicity to absolute freedom; and if, as the Guru assures us, by singing and listening to His eulogies – and so saturating ourselves with devotion – we can rid ourselves of all possible suffering:

> *gāviai suṇiai mani rakhiai bhāu* ।
> *dukhu parhari sukhu ghari lai jāī* ।।[8]

would it not be merely sensible but utterly imperative to submit to His impeccable governance unhesitatingly?

What is more, the kind of interpreting we are pleading for is of help also in looking at the divine attributes (as listed in the *Mūl Mantra*) in such a way that our understanding of God's infinite greatness, though it can never be perfect, may improve forthwith. This, however, is a point which has to be brought out at some length, partly because our suggestions in this context are very likely to deviate from the way the attributes in question have been generally interpreted – sensibly, to be sure, but generally without due concern for the way they interrelate.[9]

---

8 *Japuji, pauḍī* 5.

9 See, here, the following complaint in S. Gurbachan Singh Talib's translation of Vinoba Bhave's commentary on *Japuji:*

"Most of those who have written on *Japuji* simply list the different attributes of God provided by Guru Nanak. There is →

Presently, however, we may focus on the invocatory *Ek Oṁkār* which precedes the mention of some divine attributes. It has been suggested that in opening the *Mūl Mantra* with the sacred symbol *Ek Oṁkār*, the Guru is just *following* the hoary Indian tradition of composing religious texts.[10] But (we ask) does the Guru anywhere accept anything, be it a prevalent practice or belief, only (or even primarily) *because* it is rooted firmly in tradition? Surely, he does not. So we suggest that the invocatory *Ek Oṁkār*, signifying the oneness of God, *and* as here used by the Guru along with God's other *transcendent* attributes, may be taken primarily as a crowning truth revealed to him *as a working of His grace*; and that conformity with tradition is here just incidental. Why otherwise does the *Mūl Mantra* end with the word *Gurprasādī*? To suggest that this word, signifying the grace of God, is here simply a substitute for a words like *amen* and *tathāstu*, which have been freely used at the end of prayers or hymns – and only mean "so be it" – would be clearly to miss the Guru's unmistakable opposition to what is merely traditional.[11]

Further, as Guru Nanak himself emphasizes (as follows) Man's inability to speak (adequately) about God:

> *Who can sing His generosity?*
> *Who has the power to sing it?*

→ no attempt to see any link between the attributes."

– Translation of Vinoba Bhave's commentary on *Japuji* by S. Talib, Patiala: Publication Bureau, Punjabi University, 1980, p. 8.

10 Vinoba Bhave, *Japuji*, pp. 33-34.

11 Here, it is obvious, we disagree with Vinoba Ji.

Who can sing His kindnesses and
Know (in full) His resplendent effulgence?[12]

does it not become unavoidable to attribute the whole *mantra* (in question) to the grace of God rather than to the Guru's own (convenient) choice of just following the tradition?

At this point we find it needful to make a collateral remark. *Japuji* is not a product of sheer intellect. It is intensely spiritual, and it blazes, as it were, to show us the way to God and perfect felicity. This is why the touches of emphasis on details relating to the good life, which are quite a feature of the work, have to be traced as much to the measureless glow of that which has been revealed to him by God as to his own kindly concern (we repeat) to quell our likely incredulity in respect of what the sublime text visualizes and requires us to follow. The sublimity we speak of should be clear as we turn to interpret, at some length, the divine attributes listed in the *Mūl Mantra*.

Here, however, a question may well be put. Is not the verbal meaning of these attributes easily clear to those who know the language to which they relate? And, as in the resplendent *Ārtī*[13] (though not with the same manifest ardour) does not the Guru himself here appear simply to cherish – and surely not to interpret – the many excellences of God? So, how is it warranted to worry about the individual meanings of the attributes listed in the *Mūl Mantra*? Now, to questions such as these our answer may run as follows:

---

12 *gāvai ko tāṇu hovai kisai tāṇu* ।
gāvai ko dāti jāṇai nisāṇu ॥
– *Japuji, pauḍī* 3

13 *Sri Guru Granth Sahib*, p. 663.

True, there are two major ways of experiencing (or providing an idea of) the majesty of God: (a) in terms of images, as Guru Nanak does in the *Ārtī*, or (b) in terms of distinct attributes as has been done (by him) in the *Mūl Mantra*. But, though they are both alike warranted, what distinguishes them has to be noted with care. As we contemplate them, images such as the following:

gagan mai thālu ravi chandu dīpak baney ।[14]

here easily get interlinked because of their common realm, *gagan,* and even tend to coalesce because emission of light (in varying measure) *is common* to the sun, moon and the earthen lamps; and so keep the Guru's rapture aglow. The attributes, on the other hand (as cited in the *Mūl Mantra*), contribute individually – yet (as we hope to show) quite without mutual discord – to the glory of *kartāpurakhu*. What is more, whereas the *Ārtī* appeals to our visual imagination, the attributes, on the other hand, unite to *convey some distinct ideas*. So, as we turn to them, it will only be proper if we first distinguished their *individual meanings*, and then, if need be, so trim them (justifiably) that they may appear to cohere with or even to buttress each other.

These attributes – though they are all alike meaningful – are also dissimilar in one clear way. Two of them, namely, *kartāpurakhu* and *saibham* – are clearly positive. They mean (respectively) "the Creator of all that is there or comes to pass" and "that which is not only self-born, but creates everything out of itself".[15] The remaining four are worded negatively. *Nirbhau* and *nirvair* (respectively) mean

[14] *Sri Guru Granth Sahib*, p. 663.

[15] Vinoba Bhave, *Japuji*, p. 35.

absolutely *free from* and insusceptible to fear and enmity; *akālmūrat* signifies *freedom from* the constraints and ravages of time; and *ajūnī* means *immune* to embodiment. These negative ones are, in fact, implicit in what the positive attributes signify; and it is easy to see the point. How can that which creates everything out of itself, and is utterly self-created, be *subject to* anything? There is just no real other to it; nothing can be said to be beyond it. So it is just meaningless to speak of its being open to any influence, be it temporal – such as incarnation – or emotional, such as fear or *enmity*, the very possibility of which (i.e. *enmity*) is ruled out by the *kartā*'s *own nature as infinite love*. This, we suggest, is a little better way to interpret God's being *nirbhau* and *nirvair* than the downright assertion that God *is fearless and free from enmity*, because no one who had anything to do with religion has ever said *straightaway* (or even suspected) that "God is timorous and envious".

Later, as we turn to take a closer look at the attributes, we may have to say a good deal more about *kartāpurakhu*. But what immediately follows *ek oṁkār* in the *mūl mantra* is *satināmu*. So it would only be proper if we now gave some serious thought to these words (*satināmu*) which the Sikhs cherish happily.

By and large, these key words have been interpreted in two distinct ways: (a) His Name is True;[16] and (b) Truth is His Name.[17] Now, to turn first to (a), the moment we utter

---

[16] See, here, the following:

True is the Lord, true His Name.
(*sāchā sāhibu sāchu nāi*) – *Japuji, pauḍī* 4.

[17] Sardar Kartar Singh Duggal, *The Japuji: Sikh Morning Prayer*, p. 11.

these words, *His Name is True* meaningfully, a question crops up. His (or God's) Name, to be sure; but which particular Name of His is here meant? The question is legitimate and may not be ignored; for, in the history of our religious thought, God has surely been given different names. *Patitpāvan, dayāl, saṅkaṭamochan* are some of these. Guru Nanak himself has referred to quite a few,[18] and he has not denigrated anyone of these. What is more, a little reflection on the verbal content of the *mūl mantra* enables us to visualize some other such names, say, as follows:

Every name relates to a specific individual, thing or class of things. What is more, when we are in a laudatory frame of mind, it is easy for us – and quite acceptable – to use what is commonly regarded as an *adjective* in the way of a *noun*, as when we admire a *beautiful* maiden by exclaiming: "What a *beauty*"! Now, following this legitimate way of verbal usage, all the meaningful adjectives used in *mūl mantra* (following *satināmu*) may well be taken as names because they relate, *and can relate* only to God. But if these are taken to be names, they may all be regarded as *true* on the basis of a simple argument. In everyday life a (person's) name is taken to be true if the qualities that its verbal meaning ascribes to the individual named are truly there in him or her. In fact, it is this simple truth of reference which explains the utterance: *yathā nām tathā guṇa,* that is, parity of (a person's)

---

18 Rāma and Hari are two of these. See, here, the following:

hari nāmu dhiāiye sabadi rasu pāiye ।
vaḍbhāgi japiai hari jaso ।।
ai man meriā binu pauṛiyā mandari kiuchaḍe rām ।
aī man meriā binu beḍī pāri na ambaḍe rām ।।
– *Sri Guru Granth Sahib*, p. 1113

qualities with what his name signifies). Now, turning to the purpose in hand, the Guru is of course convinced, because it has all been revealed to him, that God is actually possessed of what the attributes (as meaningful words) ascribe to Him. Therefore, we may say, His Name, taken as anyone of these attributes, is true. Luckily, there is yet another sense, more likely to have a direct appeal to us all, in which His Name may be said to be true. His Name as our *sāhibu* is true not only because His very nature is infinite love, but because He never tires of showering His blessings on us:

> *sāchā sāhibu sāchu nāi bhākhiā bhāu apāru* ।
> *ākhahi mangahi dehi dehi dāti kare dātāru* ।।[19]

Let us now turn to the other alternative: "Truth is His Name",[20] taking *truth* specifically as "that which really is". Commitment to God *so regarded*, which *nāma-japa* both requires and conduces to, will at once prevent us from doing anything which professes or appears to be *what it is really not*. We shall abstain from thinking that mere abstention from overt speech is *real* tranquillity,[21] or that just a dip in a "holy" river is unfailingly conducive to purity of being and some gain in genuine godliness.[22] The point simply is that commitment to God as *one who really is* will generate in the true devotee a pervasive aversion to all that merely appears to be what it is really not. Conversely, where such

---

19 *Japuji, pauḍī* 4.

20 Sardar Kartar Singh Duggal, *The Japuji: Sikh Morning Prayer*, p. 11.

21 Here we are referring to the following words of the Guru: *chupai chup na hovaī je lāi rahā liv tār – Japuji, pauḍī* 1

22 *Japuji, pauḍī* 6.

commitment is missing – i.e. commitment to a God who is believed to be unquestionably there – self-deception will persist in the form of false beliefs and wrong practices. It should now be clear why Guru Nanak chooses commitment to truth as the prime discipline:

> Let Truth be thy continence; good deeds (the distinguishing) marks (of your lives); meditation of the Name thy bath.[23]

Here, what follows the first semi-colon is easy to comprehend and probably also to accept, at least for those who are steeped in traditional Indian culture. But, in so far as our present concern is with the need to interpret *sati nāmu* as "His Name is *Truth*", and collaterally also with Guru Nanak's emphasis on Truth (we repeat) as the paramount way to self-discipline, a little more may be said by way of explaining the (allegedly) absolute supremacy of Truth for the good life. M.K. Gandhi has spoken of Truth as *Ratna Chintāmaṇi.*[24] How are we to explain this emphasis on the primacy of Truth? The answer, in our view, simply is that whatever be the regulative principle of conduct that we choose to follow – may be *ahiṁsā* or *aparigraha* – it is always not only fairly possible, but needful to question if our practice of the chosen principle is *really true*. In other words, truth can easily be used as a criterion for adjudging the genuineness of any (and every) chosen direction of our endeavour to be morally better. No other yama can he granted this overriding

---

23 *sachu sanjamu karṇī kāraṇu nāvaṇu nāu japehī* |
– *Sri Guru Granth Sahib*, p. 91

24 M.K. Gandhi, *Prayer*, comp. and ed. C. Kaji, Ahmedabad: Navjeevan, p. 57.

authority to assess the propriety of the practice of the various yamas. Thus, how can the genuineness of one's (attempted) practice of *brahmacharya* be determined from the viewpoint of *aparigraha* which too is a distinct *yama*? Gandhi, we may note, even tried to verify the *truth* (or genuineness) of his attempted practice of *āsvād* – a principle (his own innovation) which requires us to abstain from *identifying ourselves* with the *taste* of the tongue, though *it* (the taste) may well be *registered* – by checking if his salivary reflex was *not* (actually / really / *truly*) activated when some eatable was put in his mouth *during the course of a fast*. So, we conclude, *without following anybody*, Guru Nanak is in very good company when he singles out the practice of Truth as the key to self-discipline, and we too (we may be allowed to add) appear justified in interpreting *satī* as Truth, and Truth as *what is really there*.

3

The Attributes Anew

IT seems to us, if a little belatedly, that so far we have not been able to give due attention to all the attributes listed in the *Mūl Mantra*. Take *kartāpurakhu*, for instance. This word is to be taken with care – i.e. not only with reference to its context, but in the light of the fact that it is a two-in-one, a coupling of *kartā* and *purakhu*. Now, to turn first to the context of the word (*kartāpurakhu*), it not only follows *ek oṁkār*, which affirms that God is one, but *satināmu* which implies, quite as clearly, that Truth is His Name.[1] Putting these two meanings together, we may say that (besides being the Creator of all that is or comes to pass) *the one God alone truly is*, and that all else comes and goes, or is ephemeral. It may be noted, in passing, that what we have just said *about God*, is vigorously asserted by the Guru himself a little after the *mantra*, as: *ādi sachu . . . hosī bhī sachu*. But, we venture to suggest, if He alone truly *is* (or eternal, that is impervious to change), the attributes that distinguish God must also be eternal and so quite otherworldly.[2] This indeed is so. The entire chain of attributes, from *nirbhau* to *saibham*, makes

---

[1] Why we prefer this interpretation of *satināmu* to "His Name is True" will be clarified a little later.

[2] Just in virtue of being eternal. The attributes that we see in the world do not float in the air. They relate to things or persons, all perishable; and therefore they disappear with their bearers.

His reality quite different from all that is human and mundane. The complete word, *kartāpurakhu*, however, calls for a little more attention. It is meant to attribute *infinite creativity* to God. But this has to be taken in such a way that His way of creating may appear to be quite unlike the way *we* bring things into being. By and large, *we* create something not only in response to some (inner or) outer stimulus, but with the help of some material which (a) we do not, as a rule, bring into being; (b) is therefore independent of us; and (c) is generally just given to us. What is more, likeable though it may well be, some *effort* is nearly always involved in our creative activity. God's creativity, on the other hand, can neither be said to involve any effort nor to depend on the supply of any external material, just because nothing *is* beyond Him.

As for *purakhu*, it is here to be taken not as suggesting masculinity but the quality of being actively causative. As Vinoba Bhave suggests, had the word *purakhu* not been used, *prakr̥ti* too could be said to be *kartā*.[3] But, we contend, simply to explain *why* the word *kartāpurakhu* has been *used* is to say nothing about what it *means*. So we suggest that God may be said to be *purakhu* (or the Prime Person) also in the sense that He is possessed of numberless specific – yet all alike infinite – attributes. Nobody will object as we speak thus. But a big question arises forthwith as we look at the matter broadly. How can we visualize God's creativity in such a way that it may appear to be utterly free from those determinants to which every act of human creativity is necessarily subject. Nothing can be said to exist independently of Him. Nor can His creativity be said to

[3] Vinoba Bhave, *Japuji*, p. 34.

involve any effort. Be it noted that such negations are not just our intrusive emphases, but are all demanded by some attributes listed in the *Mūl Mantra* itself. The last attribute, *saibham*, for instance, speaks of God as self-dependent in every way. This at once makes God's creativity impervious to all those features which characterize *our* creative ventures generally. Further, all human creation begins and ends at particular moments of time. In other words, it can never be free from subjection to time. Contrarily, God (in the *Mūl Mantra*) is emphatically declared to be *akālmūrati* – i.e. independent of the limits, distinctions and ravages of time. Finally, again because He is *akālmūrati* and *ajūnī*[4] – that is beyond the trammels not only of time but of embodiment as well – in our conception of God the suggestion of personality in the human, corporeal sense has to be studiously eschewed. This suggestion, however, is bound to look a bit too radical to be generally acceptable, because a good deal of our philosophical writing on religion has freely spoken of God, and of matters relating to Him, as *He* and *His*. What is more, if it is looked at cursorily, the word *kartāpurakhu* too appears to warrant the use of words like *He* and *His*, if only because, as a word, *purakhu* appears more or less similar to *puruṣa*. On the other hand, in the *mantra* itself there is an attribute of God, *ajūnī*, which means "immune to embodiment", and so may be taken to call for total avoidance of gender language in relation to Him. Now, how are we to get out of this conundrum? One way is to suggest that we may go on using words like *He* and *His* in relation to God, without ever forgetting that our talk is all

4 These two attributes are disparate in respect of meaning; but they are related too, because all embodiment occurs and ceases at some point of time.

along subject to an (implicitly) understood "negation" – i.e. the cautionary thought that the use of such gender language is not really apt in the context of divinity, but is only a compulsion of tradition or of our inability to find appropriate language. This suggestion, however, is clearly feeble and half-hearted, and is therefore not very likely to be generally acceptable.

We therefore venture to propose a quite new alternative. May we not interpret the attribute *kartāpurakhu* as: the Supreme *Being* regarded as the *primal creative source* of all that is there or comes to pass? Here, the word *being* signifies *reality*; and by replacing God (commonly referred to as He) with "Being Supreme" we are able to avoid all gender language totally, which (we have seen) is also a clear demand of some attributes listed in the *Mūl Mantra* itself.

Take, next, the word "*source*". Whatever is a source (of something) is surely the necessary ground – and so a cause – of that which emanates from it. Yet, as we speak thus, there is no reference, not even implicitly, to any specific effort or time. The word *primal* is even more helpful in our attempt to construe Guru Nanak's *overall* meaning. This adjective does not only mean basic, fundamental, earliest, underlying, but also *pristine*, i.e. pure, immaculate or perfect, stainless, unblemished;[5] and a God who is perfect or immaculate may well be said to create what is basically a perfect world order, imperceptible though its perfection be to our normal human intelligence. Thus it becomes credible to say that His *hukam* is utterly flawless.

---

5 Monier-Williams, *A Sanskrit–English Dictionary*, Delhi: Motilal Banarsidass, corrected edition, 2002, p. 1134.

However, the full implications of our suggestion are yet to be worked out. By replacing the divine attribute, *kartāpurakhu* with "the creative *source* of all that is", we have surely been able to avoid the suggestion not only of some effort, but also of relatedness to a specific *point* of time to which our understanding of human acts of creation is necessarily subject. But, at the same time, we have also lost a good deal of what is necessarily demanded by our commonly accepted view of *God's* creativity; and the point is easy to see. Whatever is just a *source* of what comes out of it merely spills the efflux, so to say; and this efflux – or what comes out – is already there in the source, so that nothing new is brought into being. Such cannot be the character of divine creativity. True, as the attribute *svayambhu* or *saibham* implies, God creates whatever He does wholly out of Himself, and not with the help of any external assistance. But this utterly self-dependent creativity cannot be taken as the mere projection of what is already there. It has to be regarded as a bringing into being of what is genuinely new. *Otherwise, a great deal of human creativity will come to appear clearly superior to that of God.*

Finally, if God is regarded simply as a *source* of all that is there, and not as a Person of superlative attributes and sensitiveness, how will it be possible for us to pray for His help with confidence in moments of dire suffering? The very crux of religiousness – i.e. prayer or *nāma-japa* – will disappear into vacuity. To conclude, our success in overcoming some problems that arise when we try to *understand* God's creativity *by resorting to an ingenious foray of thought* has finally resulted in annulment of the very possibility of a religious life. So, if only in the end – though not, of course, from the very beginning or totally – we have to abandon the way of sheer thinking and turn to acceptance of *śabda pramāṇa*, that is to a quiet and reverent acceptance of what the Guru's consummate spirituality has articulated in the *Mūl Mantra*. We now see, a little more clearly, the wisdom in Guru Nanak's following utterance:

sochai sochi na hovaī je sochī lakh vār ।[6]

As we know, a true devotee's communion with God, is one of faith, prayer and worship; and loving self-surrender to His goodness, supremacy and benevolence. This is amply borne out by the Guru's own attitude to God; and it is not without reason that we have ascribed Guru Nanak's *Mūl Mantra* to the grace of God. Complete self-abnegation to His authority is in fact a crowning feature of the Guru's overall communion with God. This is borne out by a careful look at his following utterances recorded in *Sri Guru Granth Sahib* at different places. Indeed, it would here be of help if we tried to visualize, though not without some diffidence, Guru Nanak's overall relatedness to God on the basis of his own following utterances:

> You (alone) kill and rejuvenate us. You forgive us and (even) (allow us to) merge ourselves in your self. You alone inspire us to chant your Name.[7]

---

6 "By mere pondering, man cannot have a (satisfactory) conception of God, even though he may ponder over lacs of time" – *Japuji, pauḍī* 1.

7 *Sri Guru Granth Sahib*, p. 154:
tū māri jivālahi bakhasi milaī ।
jiu bhāvī tiu nāmu japāī ।।

This monumental utterance, we may note, is neither a dispassionate report on a matter of fact nor just easy accordance with what might have been asserted by other saints, but a personal testament emanating from lifelong devoutness and self-denying faith. This is borne out more clearly by the following categorical utterance:

> I have entrusted my body and mind to Him, and so I neither fear death nor am longing to live.[8]

However, such awareness of God's (beneficient) control over human beings in general, as also over his own birth and death, is not everything about Guru Nanak's awareness of God's sovereignty. He is also convinced of the fact that it is God who controls the elements, and has staged the whole drama of the world on His own. Nor is this awareness just the cool recognition of an impersonal truth. As is quite manifest in the scintillating *Ārtī*, the awareness in question is (at its most intense) a rapturous luxuriating in the *insightful* faith that the rhythm and beauty that characterize the play of elements and disposition of the heavenly bodies are just a kind of ode to His glory.

Here, however, we have to mark a difference. The Guru of course exults in contemplating the beauty of the heavens and the play of elements, but he does not do so in the way of a poet, say, like Wordsworth, whose (own) heart (alone) "leaps up" when he beholds "a rainbow in the sky". To Guru Nanak, indeed, the whole variegated expanse of nature is not merely his personal paean to God's majesty, but an abiding blessing *for one and all*. A yet clearer index of the Guru's

---

8 *Sri Guru Granth Sahib*, p. 20:

tanu manu gur pahi vechiā manu dīā sirū nāli . . . ।
marṇai kī chintā nahi jīvan ki nahi ās ॥

own humility and *self-subjugation to* His benevolence for the sake of redemption from multifarious sinfulness, which inhibits spiritual progress all along, is provided by the following:

> *jetā samundu sāgaru nīri bhariā*
> *tete avguṇ hamāre* ।
> *daiyā karahu kichhu mihar*
> *upāvahu ḍubde patthar tāre* ॥[9]

Now, how are we to interpret the first two lines of this penitent prayer sensibly? At first sight they appear hyperbolic. But the trouble is that Guru Nanak is not the only saint to resort to such seemingly inflated language. Sūrdās goes to the extent of declaring that no one can equal him in viciousness and lechery.[10]

Tulsīdās too speaks of himself as a well-known sinner (*prasiddh pātakī*[11]), Mīrā Bāī roundly dismisses herself as *patit*[12] (depraved). Surely, none of these luminaries in the field of devoutness – all alike blessed with a good measure of poetic skill as well – can be accused of wilful

---

9 *Sri Guru Granth Sahib*, p. 156.

10 Here the reference is to that well-known *bhajan* of Sūrdās which opens as follows:

mo sam kaun kuṭil khal kāmī

11 The reference, here, is to the following lines in a Tulsīdās *bhajan*:

> *tu dayāl dīn haun, tū dātā haun bhikhārī* ।
> *haun prasiddh pātakī, tu pāp-puñj hārī* ॥

12 This is borne out by the very opening two words of the second line in the following:

main hari patit pāvan suney
main patit tum patit pāvan,
dou bānak baney – Mīrā Bāī

untruthfulness or mistaken reporting. What then is the way to make sense of such apparent self-belittlement? Luckily, some clue is here provided by the opening words in the following soliloquy of Gandhi:

> *It is an unbroken torture to me* that I am still far from Him who governs every breath of my life, and whose offspring I am.[13]

Here, a careful look at the italicized words can be taken to make for a helpful simile. Just as a grievously ill and hospitalized cancer patient not only pines for instant relief from his insufferable pain, but finds it very difficult to bear the slightest delay in the ministration of the palliative medicine, similarly – just because it hampers what a saint longs and lives for, i.e. ever greater closeness to God – even a minuscule native human weakness can be felt as a gigantic impediment; and the collateral delay, as a stretch of infinity. *What here appears overblown to us is possibly a very real discomfiture to* those who are intensely devout. We see no other way to make sense of the saints' enigmatic utterances we have cited.

As for the Guru's own devoutness, it is a blend of quite a few hues, so to say; and to see how multifarious it is we have to unravel the variety it embraces. Here, we may begin by turning anew to the *Mūl Mantra* which provides a fitting preamble to *Japuji*. As we have already said, it is clearly an impressive utterance of revelatory knowledge which Guru Nanak is just blessed with, as a gift of His grace (here again, we may add, we go by the word *gurprasādī*). And if it has

---

13 M.K. Gandhi, *An Autobiography or Story of My Experiments with Truth.*

been hailed as a *Mūl Mantra*, it is because of two reasons. First, it relates entirely to God who is commonly regarded as the basic reality, and, second, revelatory knowledge, which the *mantra* in question may be taken to provide, has been generally regarded as the primal vehicle of ultimate truth.

However, there are quite a few individual faiths too which show the Guru as related to God varyingly; illumine his being and speech unmistakably; and also bespeak his personal sensitiveness to traditional wisdom. Some of these credos, strewn all over *Japuji*, may be listed as follows:

> *nānak nirguṇi guṇu kare guṇvantiā guṇu de* ।
> *tehā koi na sujhaī je tisu guṇu koi kare* ।।[14]

God, says Guru Nanak, can condescend to shower some excellence even on those who are quite plain beings; and what is more (in so far as He is *guṇanidhāna*) He can also add to the merits of those who are already worthy. But (the Guru continues) it is impossible to vizualize anyone who could add to *God's* excellences (because they are already limitless). An addition is possible only in respect of that which is limited. His excellences cannot be comprehended adequately:

> *sochai sochi na hovaī je sochī lakh vār* ।[15]

This utterance echoes the view of saints and sages in general. It declares that, howsoever it may try, thought can never capture the full reality of God. Guru Nanak reiterates this truth in the light of his own experience:

> *je hau jāṇā ākhā nāhī*[16]

[14] *Japuji, pauḍī* 7.

[15] Ibid., *pauḍī* 1.

[16] Ibid., *pauḍī* 5.

This utterance may be interpreted as follows: "Even though I have known God – say, by way of intimate, personal experience – I cannot *describe* Him. God is ineffable, quite beyond words".

Here, however, a distinction has to be kept in mind. Guru Nanak does not wish to say that we cannot *at all* speak of, or use words in relation to God. In the *Mūl Mantra* he himself has used quite a few adjectives, all meaningful words, in respect of God. So his overall view could only be that mere thinking and use of language *cannot quite seize the reality of God in its entirety.*

sabhnā jiā kā iku dātā so mai visari na jāī ।[17]

Here, the Guru does not only articulate the common faith of those who are deeply religious – the faith that God is the source of all life; but also aspires to imbibe the truth as one of his vital, undeviating faiths.

All in all, the devoutness that Guru Nanak pleads for (and is himself saturated with) is absolute. It is not merely an enchantment of the ear, produced by listening to devotional songs (*śravaṇa*), but a godward orientation of one's entire mentality:

nānak gāviai guṇī nidhānu ।
gāviai suṇiai mani rakhiai bhāu ।।[18]

---

17 *Japuji, pauḍī* 5.

18 Ibid.

4

The "How" and "Why" of Devotion

How the two poetic lines (just cited) provide a sanctifying preface to Guru Nanak's entire treatment of *śravaṇa, manan* and *nididhyāsana*[1] calls for some detailed thinking, and so we may defer it to a later stage of enquiry. For the present let us deal with a more basic question. What has Guru Nanak to say on the "how" and "why" of devotion? Why should we at all take to the path of godliness, and what exactly is the way? Now, a very clear answer to these questions is implicit in the following lines which occur not once, but repeatedly – i.e. at the end of every *pauḍī* from the eight to eleventh one:

> *nānak bhagtā sadā vigāsu* ।
> *suṇiai dūkh pāp kā nāsu* ॥[2]

What these lines say is easy to put. Those who are truly devout are always brimming with cheer; and the reason for their perennial felicity is that genuine commitment to the

1 In all probability, this particular word has not been used by Guru Nanak. His own equivalent for it may be said to be provided by *mani rakhiai bhāu*.

2 Ibid., *pauḍī*s 8-11.

Name of God (regarded as *nirañjan*[3] or perfectly *pure*), imbues them with a penchant for what is proper and good; eradicates the very tendency to transgress the norms of good conduct; and so obviates all such suffering[4] as is caused by our normal foibles. The same laudable commitment is related to yet another happy consequence in the last two lines which close every *pauḍī* from the twelfth to the fifteenth. These lines declare that those (alone) who are given to devout contemplation (or *manan*) of the Name of God (as *nirañjan*) come to realize the full compass of its significance. *Manan,* we are told, makes for intense mental attunement which leads ultimately to instantaneous illumination, as distinguished from struggling, piecemeal thinking:

> *mannai surati hovai mani budhi* |[5]

We may now turn to the second question. What is the right way to cultivate devoutness? Here, in incidental accordance with the traditional Indian view, Guru Nanak recommends a threefold discipline: *śravaṇa, manan* and *nididhyāsana.*[6] *Śravaṇa* or listening to songs of devotion (*śabad*s) – as also (may be) to some elderly saints' accounts of the amazingly gratifying results, brought about in their long personal lives simply by holding on to prayer and faith even in calamitous times – has been put as the very first step in the triple

---

[3] *aisā nāmu nirañjanu hoi* |
je ko manni jāṇai mani koi ||
–*Japuji, pauḍī*s 12-15

[4] Physical and psychological.

[5] *Japuji, pauḍī* 13.

[6] Our use of this word here, in respect of Guru Nanak, is more or less tentative. A little more that is needed in this connection has been said later.

discipline, simply because listening to both devotional *songs* and the heartening assurances of saints can easily enthral the mind of nascent devotees. Music, of course, has its own intrinsic charm, but the kindly verbal exhortations of genuine saints can also carry conviction. Words that relate to objects can surely make for clear understanding; but those that appear to emanate from genuine saints' personal realization of spiritual truths are not merely understood, but at once tend to serve as a gentle, but effective prod to turn away from a life of sheer worldliness to the path of devoutness, partly because when they actually make the verbal appeal, the saints' very visage bespeaks sincerity. Word that arises from the very depths of one's being is its own testament; and as we have just outlined it, *śravaṇa* can indeed easily induce listeners to think devoutly of God, and of His greatness and glory. What is more, this process may well continue indefinitely, if only because God's own attributes (and, we add, their ways of relating to human situations) are both numberless, and so make it possible for us to keep Him continually in mind. See here the following:

> *nānak gāviai guṇī nidhānu* ।
> *gāviai suṇiai mani rakhiai bhāu* ॥[7]

The first line here does not specify any particular attribute of God, such as *kṛpānidhān* or *patitpāvan*, but speaks of Him as a repository of numberless attributes. This is why our *manan* or devout *contemplation* of God's excellences can go on interminably and so defy estimation:

---

[7] *Japuji, pauḍī* 5.

mannai kī gati kahī na jāi ।
je ko kahai pichhai pachhutāi ॥[8]

At the same time, *manan* (we are told) makes for a growing realization of the glory of God's Name:

aisā nāmu nirañjanu hoi ।
je ko manni jāṇai mani koi ॥[9]

Here, however, a question may well be put. If *manan* generally tends to be an endless process, how can anyone pass on from *its* practice to (what may be called) *nididhyāsana*[10] which calls for a (more or less) riveting contemplation of some specific attribute(s) of God? To this, we believe, an answer can be improvised on the basis of what is implicit in some of Guru Nanak's own utterances, such as the following:

sabhnā jīā kā iku dātā so mai visari na jāī ॥[11]

sāchā sāhibu sāchu nāi bhākhiā bhāu apāru ॥[12]

ākhahī mangahi dehi dehi dāti kare dātāru ॥[13]

All these encomia speak of God not only as the originator of all life, but as our supreme benefactor. So, following the Guru himself, in (what is generally called) *nididhyāsana* we

---

8 Ibid., *pauḍī* 12.

9 Ibid.

10 As we have already said, Guru Nanak himself does not use exactly this particular word. His equivalent for this word (we repeat) is probably provided by the following: *mani rakhīe bhāu*.

11 *Japuji, pauḍī*s 5, 6.

12 Ibid., *pauḍī* 4.

13 Ibid.

may well fix our minds on God as *dātāru* or as ever loving and supremely benevolent. True, this word, *dātāru*, signifying the *Giver*, stands for just one attribute of God; but this is exactly what *nididhyāsana* demands – i.e. a passage from a ceaseless flitting of the mind across different attributes of God to an unswerving commitment to just one of these. Here, however, we may also note that, as Guru Nanak uses it, the word *dātāru* does not mean a donor in the everyday sense, but one who (a) not only *gives* life to one and all[14] (b) never tires of granting our genuine prayers;[15] and, what is more, (c) whose very way of dealing with us is love.[16] The word *dātāru* is therefore so richly suggestive of God's ceaseless benevolence that it at once touches the heart, and so may well induce us to lean towards God in loving subservience. Be it noted that this epithet (*dātāru*) is quite different from attributes like *akālmūrat* and *ajūnī*. These unfamiliar words, which distinguish the *Mūl Mantra*, have to be *understood*, perhaps not without some effort. On the other hand, *benevolence*, which is clearly implicit in the meaning of *dātāru*, is a quality which appeals to us readily, and which we are all familiar with. Indeed the single thought that He is our only all-time benefactor is enough to capture the heart and to serve as the superlative anchor for our practice of (what may be called) *nididhyāsana*.[17] This,

14 *Guru Granth Sahib*, English and Punjabi tr. Manmohan Singh, Amritsar: Shiromani Gurdwara Prabandhak Committee, 7th edn., 2004, vol. 1, p. 4.

15 *Japuji, pauḍī* 4.

16 Ibid.

17 Here, again, we are using this word with reserve. Why we say so should be clear in the light of relevant remarks we have already made earlier, as footnotes.

however, is not everything about the matter we are dealing with. What is yet to be noted is the fact that a sublime ring of altruistic concern distinguishes Guru Nanak's own impeccable devoutness. If he rejoices, as he certainly does, in his consummate love of the Name (of God), and extols this commitment as the supreme goal of life,[18] it is not merely because it has made *his own life* blissful, but because (he believes that) it is God who has all along lent value to the lives of all those who have finally distinguished themselves as *pīr*s and *siddh*s by listening to the chanting of His name not only soulfully, but perennially:

suṇiai sidh pīr suri nāth ||[19]

This emphasis on the redemptive power of God becomes more explicit from the twentieth *pauḍī* onward. In this context, however, Guru Nanak makes quite a few references to some spiritual truths which are a bit too subtle for us, and which, by and large, we can only allude to, reverentially. At the same time, they cannot be totally ignored. So, with a view to making them a little intelligible we may proceed as follows, in terms of individual points:

(a) The very opening of the twentieth *pauḍī* declares that if one's sense of values has gone awry – may be because of association with people of low morals – the only way to redeem it from depravity is to try to cultivate an ever-deepening love of His Name:

---

18 Because it puts a final end to all our evil-doing and suffering. *Japuji, pauḍī*s, 8-11.

19 Ibid., *pauḍī* 8.

bharīai mati pāpā kai saṅgi ।
ohu dhopai nāvai kai raṅgi ॥[20]

Now, what one is here required to do will become easier to accomplish if God, as symbolized by the Name, is thought of as *nirañjan,*[21] i.e. as being utterly beyond the spell of *māyā* and so impervious to worldly evils.

(b) It may here be added, incidentally, that for Guru Nanak the only worthwhile pilgrimage is purification of one's inner being:

antargati tīrathi mali nāu ।[22]

Vinoba Bhave here draws an interesting parallel. What the Guru speaks of as (*antargati tīrath*) has been called *mānastīrth* by Śaṅkarāchārya.[23]

(c) The last four lines of the twenty-first *pauḍī* run as follows:

---

[20] Ibid., *pauḍī* 20.

An interesting parallel of what reference no. 1 and 4 here say is provided by the following poetic lines of Mīrā Bāī.

rāmnām rasa pījai manvā
taja kusaṅg satsaṅg baithā nit
hari charchā sun līje ।
kām krodh mad lobh moha ko
bahā chitta saun dīje ॥

[21] *aisā nāmu nirañjanu hoi – Japuji, pauḍī*s 12-15.

[22] *Japuji, pauḍī* 21.

[23] Vinoba Bhave, *Japuji,* p. 65.

sabhi guṇ tere mai nāhī koi ।
viṇu guṇ kīte bhagati na hoi ।
suasati āthi bāṇī barmāu ।
sati suhāṇu sadā mani chāu ।।[24]

Here, the very first line speaks of God as the one true source of all (primal[25]) qualities, and it is clearly akin to the following utterance of the Guru which occurs in the seventh *pauḍī*:

nānak nirguṇi guṇu kare guṇvantiā guṇu de ।[26]

However, what the second of the *four* lines of the twenty-first *pauḍī* cited above – *viṇu . . . na hoi* – say cannot be accepted without question. It declares that no genuine *bhakti* is possible without the due cultivation of (some requisite) qualities. But here a question may well be put. Is the required acquisition of qualities expected to occur *before* taking to the path of *bhakti*? Or is it supposed to run *along with* the practice of devotion? Obviously, the two have to go together. In fact, the very decision to cultivate love of God is at once some turning away from sheer lure of the world; a step on the way to growing self-control, and so a lift in one's sense of values, if only a slight and initial one.

Here, however, Guru Nanak makes a concrete and helpful suggestion. It would become easier, he observes, to acquire the qualities in question if the Name that we recite in *japa* were regarded as *brahma vāṇī* – as relating to the One

---

24 *Japuji, pauḍī* 21.

25 Primal or highest (ethereal), as distinguished from subsidiary, mundane qualities such as warmth in greeting visitors which cannot be equated with God's perennial love for us all.

26 *Japuji, pauḍī* 7.

who is at once the finality of truth, goodness and *bliss*. This is indeed the emphasis where the Guru speaks thus:

> *suasati āthi bāṇī barmāu* ।
> *sati suhāṇu sadā mani chāu* ॥[27]

What these two lines mean may be clarified by attending, as follows, to the individual meanings of the words they comprise. *Bāṇi barmāu* may here be taken to signify *brahma vāṇī*; and the remaining words may be interpreted as follows:[28]

suasati	Well-being, prosperity
sati	Of the nature of Truth
suhāṇu	Auspicious
sadā mani chāu	Ever pleasing to the mind

Commitment to God so regarded may well be expected to hearten the devotee with the *thought* that He is ever there (or is *sat*) to provide for his welfare and happiness. Be it noted, however, that it is not only the *thought* in question which will here provide the sustenance needed, but God Himself as well. He is not only *guṇanidhān* – intrinsically an infinity of excellences – but is ever ready to let us benefit from them, provided we turn to Him in truth and humility, essentially because He is benevolent by nature (*dātāru*). If, as Guru Nanak declares, He can lavish qualities even on those who are very ordinary beings,[29] will He not provide the needed purity and perseverance to those who strive

---

27 Ibid., *pauḍī* 21.

28 Ibid. Here, in translating the words listed we have played safe by following Vinoba Bhave.

29 *Japuji, pauḍī* 7: *nānak nirguṇi guṇu kare* ।

valiantly to tread and hold on to the path of *bhakti* (or devotion)? Be that as it may, the best of all *sādhnā*s (self-disciplines) is commitment to, and love of God; and, in Guru Nanak's view, anyone who tries to fashion his own independent approach to Him is bound to come to grief.[30] On our own we cannot even initiate our godly uplift. It is God alone who excites in us an urge to turn to Him worshipfully. This is indeed a blessing of His; and it is of basic value because it is this which can finally make for attainment of *mokṣa*.

Between these two ends, however – i.e. from the earliest impulse to turn to God to the attainment of *mokṣa* – our devoutness can vary appreciably in intensity. Some become so intensely devoted to God that they can welcome even a calamity as a blessing of His grace:

> *ketiā dūkh bhūkh sad mār* ।
> *ehi bhi dāti teri dātār* ।।[31]

How are these two lines to be interpreted satisfactorily? How can a calamity, which may cause us not mere inconvenience but excruciating anguish, ever be welcome? Luckily, an answer can here be improvised in the light of the mental make-up of an individual who is genuinely religious. In the conduct of everyday life he may also be fairly successful, besides having a more or less steadfast faith in the supremacy of God's will. Now, when (in real life) he *is* able to achieve, say, what he has been eagerly wanting to, he may well be

---

30 *je ko khāiku ākhaṇi pāi* ।
ohu jāṇai jetīā muhi khāi ।।
– *Japuji, pauḍī* 25

31 *Japuji, pauḍī* 25.

tempted to think that here God has graciously permitted the effort of his will to succeed. In other words, at this happy moment *God's* will may be taken to coincide with his own, *and so to remain eclipsed* and *unmarked*. Contrarily, when his own human efforts fail to remedy an intense personal suffering, he may well be able to steady himself – because he is devout too – with the thought that it is *God's supreme will* that has barred the way; and that it has thus become manifest to his eye of faith, and so provides an occasion to rejoice, rather than to fret and fume. This, we believe, is the crystal of truth, so to say, in the seemingly enigmatic utterance, voiced by some Sufi saints (in their own language):

> Our dark days reflect the glory of God.

There is however one other way, and more obviously in accord with the Guru's own utterances in *Japuji,* in which the point we have just tried to make can be argued sensibly. We may put it simply as follows:

> Nothing happens without or beyond His *hukam*. Further, His *hukam* is unqualifiedly and eternally benevolent. Therefore, the calamity that we may be facing presently must *somehow* conduce to our welfare ultimately, though we (as we are) may not be able to see how this is going to come about. So, just as a demand of faith, the calamity in question should be welcome or at least quietly endured.

Be that as it may, Guru Nanak sees the working of God's benevolent will in everything that happens, and so not only in the dawn of devotion, but in its culmination as *mokṣa*. At the same time, he does not fail to emphasize the importance of individual human effort. He declares unmistakably that everyone gets what he really deserves, in virtue of the quality of his own conduct though of course within (and because of) the working of His *hukam.*[32]

This indeed is why Guru Nanak distinguishes and emphasizes[33] the individual steps of the psycho-ethical discipline that finally enables one to "mint" such words of impeccable spiritual wisdom as can lend depth and fervour to our endeavour to come closer to God. At the same time, however, he also insists that the effort in question should aim at transcending the sense of our own importance in self-effacing love of God, not at comprehending what He is or how exactly His ethereal qualities operate in life's varying situations. In this context, however, two additional points have to be borne in mind.

First, though beginning with the opening *Mūl Mantra*, Guru Nanak himself ascribes (subsequently) quite a few additional attributes to God, none of these attributes is regarded as having determinate *limits*. This is true as much of the basic attribute *sat* as of the other qualities. The Guru, we have seen, insists that God *is* not only there presently, but has been there since eternity, and will abide for ever.[34] Second, he is just as emphatic on the limitlessness of God's benevolence:

dedā de laide thaki pāhi ǀ[35]

---

[32] *āpe bīji āpe hi khāhu* ǀ
nānak hukmī āvahu jāhu ǀǀ – *Japuji, pauḍī* 20

[33] Quite explicitly – and even serially – in thirty-eighth *pauḍī*, for instance.

[34] *ādi sachu jugādi sachu* ǀ
hai bhi sachu nānak hosī bhī sachu ǀǀ

[35] *Japuji, pauḍī* 3.

In fine, none of God's attributes, though they are all alike determinate in meaning, is thought of as having a limited range. Here, incidentally, it would be relevant if we give some thought to a specific question. In Guru Nanak's view, is God *saguṇa* or *nirguṇa*? Now, going by what we find *in Japuji* – with which alone we are primarily concerned – our answer has to be straightaway. *Saguṇa*, and we can argue for our answer as follows:

(a) The Guru is categorical in maintaining that the best way to realize God is to cultivate an evergrowing love for Him. Now, this is possible only if God is regarded as *saguṇa*. This is indeed the compelling evidence not only of those saints who have been known for their devoutness, but even of *average men and women* who occasionally try to pray, however perfunctorily. They have got to think, if not really to believe steadfastly, that He not only listens to, but is sensitive and sympathetic to their prayers. Now, so to think is at once to regard Him as *saguṇa*.

(b) What is more, the very opening of *Japuji* is nothing, if not a rapid mention of His attributes. A *guṇa*, as we know, is a quality, attribute, property, or *peculiarity*.[36] Being quite without shape – i.e. *niraṅkār* (or *nirākār*) – is as much a *guṇ* as *benevolence*. So, the view that God is *niraṅkār* does not at all collide with the thought that He is *saguṇa*.

What is more, in ascribing some specific *guṇa*s to God, Guru Nanak is clearly insistent. One of these is benevolence. Thus, see the following:

---

36 Monier-Williams, *Sanskrit–English Dictionary*, p. 357.

ākhahi mangahi dehi dehi dāti kare dātāru – *pauḍī* 4
sabhnā jīā kā iku dātā . . . – *pauḍī* 5

Nor is it here irrelevant to note that, in *Japuji*, God is explicitly spoken of as the source of all *guṇas*:

sabhi guṇ tere . . . – *pauḍī* 21
nānak nirguṇī guṇu kare . . . – *pauḍī* 7

(c) Above all, Guru Nanak also roundly characterizes God as *guṇī nidhānu*, i.e. as a repository of qualities (*pauḍī* 5).

All this is easy to follow. But there is (in this context) a good deal of dictum in *Japuji* which calls for some hard thinking. Consider, for instance, the Guru's emphasis that though God Himself is the highest reality, His Name is even higher:

vaḍā sāhibu ūchā thāu ।
ūche upari ūchā nāu ॥[37]

Now, how can this be explained? How can anything be higher than God, admittedly the superlative reality? Here, we suggest, the Guru's own emphasis on *nāma-japa* can be used to make for an answer. The view that God *is* the highest reality may well be *accepted* as true in itself; but He actually *becomes* our cherished destiny only when we take to reciting *His Name* with devotional fervour. In other words, it is His Name which makes God directly relevant to our need for happiness and relief. It is from this patently human point of view that His Name may be said to be superior to His reality.

The same happy conclusion can be reached in one other way. Every real object of thought has two aspects. It is a

---

[37] *Japuji, pauḍī* 24.

that and a *what*. In other words, it is not only there as an existent, but has a definite character. Now, the various names in terms of which we love and worship God, such as *patitpāvan* and *kr̥pānidhān* all invest God with definite attributes, make Him *saguṇa* and so ador*able*, though (as we have already said) not comprehensible, because the extent *and actual working* of these attributes in life's varying situations are both alike unfathomable.

Yet, when everything has been said by way of glorifying *nāma-japa*, a basic question remains. What exactly is this famed devotional practice? One simple answer may be put thus: *Japa* is the repetitive and *devout* recitation of His Name. This Name can vary. It may be Rāma,[38] Hari,[39] or simply God. But in every case it has got to be devout, instead of being a merely vocal utterance. Further, where it is properly done – i.e. as a definite fillip to godliness – it is not merely occasional but tends to be repetitive and habitual. If in a moment of intense agony one just blurts out: *hey bhagavān* (O God!), it is not *japa* at all, though an utterance of His Name it admittedly is. Even Gandhi's last minute "Hey Rāma" is not *japa*, though intensely devout and self-effacing it may well have been. What is even more necessary for effective *japa* is the devotee's *unremitting endeavour to deepen his love of God*. Ideally, every utterance of His Name has to

---

38 *jiare rām japat manu mānu* ǀ *antari lāgī jali bujhi pāiā gurmukhi giānu* ǁ – *Sri Guru Granth Sahib*, p. 20

39 (a) *hari japi jīare chhūṭiae gurmukhi chīnae āpu* ǀ – Ibid.

(b) *hari simari ekāṅkār sāchhā sabhu jagati jini upāiā* ǀ – Ibid., p. 1113

(c) *sakhā sainu piāru, prītamu nāmu hari kā japo* ǀ – Ibid.

feel as a longing to get ever closer to Him, and to get rid of one's innate moral foibles, along with unshaken faith in His power to liberate us, as also in His exhaustless benevolence. Intenseness of yearning is here the key requisite. This indeed is what the Guru wishes to emphasize where he speaks thus:

> Just as it is the heat of fire that makes one metal melt into another, so it is the *bhakta's own* intensely fervent devotion which can enable him to shed the sense of his own individual identity in God-consciousness.[40]

It may appear to us, however, that this specific emphasis on the devotee's individual effort does not quite square with Guru Nanak's own following utterance which too appears categorical:

> *Thou taketh and giveth life,*
> *And forgiving* (*also*) *unitest us with Thee,*
> *And, as is Thy will, so one meditateth*
> *On Thy Name.*[41]

If, as the two closing lines just cited clearly say, our recourse to, and persistence in *nāma-japa* both depend on His sweet will, what is the point in *our* being exhorted to make our yearning for God red-hot as the first quote requires us to? To this our answer readily is that though the initial impulse

---

[40] *dhātu milai phuni dhātu kau siftī sifati samāī*
lālu, gulālu, gahbarā sachā rañgu chaḍāū
sachu milai santokhiā, hari japi aikai bhāi – Sri Guru Granth Sahib, p. 18

[41] *tu māri jivālahi bakhsi milāi* ।
jiu bhāvi tiu nāmu japāī – Sri Guru Granth Sahib, p. 154
– Tr. Gopal Singh, *Sri Guru Granth Sahib* (English version), vol. I, Delhi: Gurdas Kapur and Sons, 1960.

to take to *nāma-japa* may well *be* His gift, this surely does not make it unnecessary that we too may be exhorted continually – say, by saints and *haricharchā* generally – to hold on to the path valiantly, *because the numberless human foibles to which we are all subject cannot be rubbed out all at once.*

Further, simply taking His Name, even repeatedly – and may be also with a little feeling – is not quite enough. We have to ponder freely not only on His fairness in giving us unfailingly the kind of embodiment (and ascent in goodness) we deserve by virtue of the quality of our actual conduct, but also His gracious readiness to grant us – again, if we merit it – liberation from the birth–death cycle:

> *amṛt velā sachu nāu vaḍiāī vīchāru* ।
> *karamī āvai kapḍā nadarī mokhu duāru* ॥[42]

Guru Nanak himself not only resorts to, but even glories in contemplating God's goodness and majesty, and *bemoans his own finitude* which is heightened by the very thought of His superlative attributes.[43] Now, this may look a little odd to us, for the Guru's spiritual eminence is utterly beyond question. Luckily, however, we can think of a rough parallel which may temper the seeming oddity a little. The abler an intellectual becomes in dealing with niceties of thought and language, the greater may be his sense of lingering inadequacy in either direction. A genuine devotee, however, is here better placed. His very impatience with the

---

[42] *Japuji, pauḍī* 4.

[43] *merey sāhibā kauṇu jāṇai guṇ terey* ।
kaheyna jānī auguṇ merey ॥
– *Sri Guru Grath Sahib*, p. 156

unrelenting clutch of finitude may at once be a quiet prayer for release; and this will itself be a step towards the cherished goal. The intellectual, on the other hand, has to rest on his own prowess; and if it helps, it may lead to a furtive rise in his sense of self-importance, relieved (maybe) by some conscious, staccato moments of struggle to avoid feeling smug over his achievements. The Guru, on the other hand, recommends absolute submission to, and dependence on His authority, if one is to replenish his days and nights with abiding bliss:

> *praṇvati nānaku hukmu pachhaṇai* ।
> *sukhu hovai dinu rāti* ॥[44]

Yet, impressive though such assurances are – not only because of the sublimity of what they require us to do, but also because of the ready appeal of what they promise in return, *nāma-japa* is by no means an easy path to tread. A problem crops up also when we try to *understand* its actual run; and it is likely to trouble those in particular who look at it all as inquisitive outsiders. The point, however, has to be clarified; and we may do it as follows.

If it be taken as a distinct discipline, which it really is, the actual recitation of His Name (as *nāma-japa*) is neither a single utterance nor a bleak, undivided stretch. It is rather a running series of quite a few emphases, vocalized or just cherished quietly, even soulfully. A *pervasive devoutness* is its very life. In everyday life, on the other hand, we think of God and His attributes – such as benevolence and omnipotence – sincerely only when we are faced with such

---

[44] *Sri Guru Grath Sahib*, p. 156.

tough situations as we cannot manage on our own. The *thought* of some of these attributes – such as *sāhibu* (4th *pauḍī*), *dātā* (5-6th *pauḍī*s), *nirañjan* (12th *pauḍī*), which are all bearers of *specific* meanings – may also tend to adhere to the (devout) individual utterances of the Name that make the actual run of *japa*. Now, bearing in mind both these ways of being concerned with God, a question may well be put. How does it become possible to save the *running* devoutness, which (as we have said) is the very life-breath of genuine *nāma-japa*, from being ruffled by the *specificity* of the attributes, the thought of which (we repeat) may cling to the individual utterances of *nāma* that make the content of *japa*? The answer is: it all depends on how effervescent one's devoutness is. To one whose heart is ablaze with devotion *during nāma-japa* (or even generally, as is the case with Guru Nanak), no attribute is merely *understood*. It is rather felt at once as a moment of soulful swell to get closer to God; and therefore, far from being disturbed, the run of devoutness is here only enlivened. Two good illustrations of the point we are trying to make may here be cited; one (a) relating to Guru Nanak; and the other (b) to Mīrā Bāī:

(a) *sabhnā jīā kā iku dātā so mai visari na jāī* (5th *pauḍī*)

(b) *mai hari patitpāvan sunai* ।
mai patit tum patitpāvan doū bānak baney ॥

Here in (a) the *thought* of His being the Giver of all life (*dātā*), clearly an attribute, is at once relieved of its sheer *objectivity* by the *overrunning* ebullience of a self-induced prayer for remembering Him eternally; and in (b) the thought of His being an unfailing redeemer – again an acknowledged attribute of God – is made the basis of a loving – yet (a) little logical (?) – argument which may be taken to taper off into a wordless, yet insistent prayer for redemption, even as the quiet plaintive look of a woebegone dependent may itself serve as a prayer for instant relief. Here (in respect of (b)) the whole point may be put clearly as follows. "*You* are said to be the saviour of the lowly. I am a fallen one already. *So, why do you not redeem me forthwith*"? Here, the (italicized) insistence is implicit.

This indeed is why Guru Nanak requires us to *intensify our love of God maximally*, through ruthless self-discipline. There is no other way to check *thought* from disturbing the requisite evenness of sentience during *nāmajapa*, for we just cannot think without making distinctions.

The Guru, we may note, does not merely *enjoin* that we should cultivate unremitting and ever deeper faith (*mani rakhīe bhāu*). He also takes care to provide the requisite inducement which is both winsome and valid. His categorical assertion that limitless love alone is His language or way of governing our world[45] is quickly followed (we have seen) by the generous assurance that by cultivating implicit faith in God one can secure perfect individual happiness and riddance from suffering.[46]

Yet, we may note, sublime and hence difficult to comprehend though His attributes truly are, they do nothing to alienate God from us. They rather make Him accessible, by providing something that we can hold on to, in our struggle to cultivate faith. Nor is there any risk of going astray if we choose some *specific* attribute as our main avenue to faith. What can serve to keep us streadfast in every such

---

45 *bhākhiā bhāu apāru – Japuji, pauḍī* 4

46 *dukhu parhari sukhu ghari lai jāī – Japuji, pauḍī* 5

case of exclusive commitment is unremitting and intense devoutness. Luckily, the point we are trying to make here may be clarified by drawing on Guru Nanak's own proclivity for *rāga* music. During the actual process of unfolding the canvas of a *rāga* (or melody-type) a vocalist can easily tarry at – and even intensify – the singing of an individual *svara* without for a moment forgetting the general form of the *rāga* which embraces the note in question. So nothing really prevents adherence to some select attribute of God from serving as an implicit reminder of His overall exaltation, provided the person resorting to it is suffused with devotion.

This possibility, however, should not make us indifferent to Guru Nanak's emphasis on the otherworldly uniqueness of God's attributes. Consider, in this context, *pauḍī* 26 which is an ecstatic, yet consistent account of God's superlative, and inestimable qualities. Here is a part of the way it runs:

> *amulu bakhsīs amulu nīsāṇu* ।
> *amulu karamu amulu phurmāṇu* ।।
> *amulo amulu ākhiā na jāi* ।
> *ākhi ākhi rahey liv lāi* ।।[47]

The reference here is to His benevolence, in the main. It is fairly easy to have an idea of a *man's* benevolence, say, by counting the number of charitable institutions he finances yearly. But can we ever come to the end of counting God's blessings? He gives us our very life – to us all, with our multifarious capacities,[48] including the overtopping abilities

---

[47] *Japuji, pauḍī* 26.

[48] "It is He who gives life to all, that gives power and being to all that exists" – Mother Teresa, *Everything Starts from Prayer: A Full Circle Book*, 2nd repr., 2007, p. 46.

not only to make our everyday living hassle-free, but even to attain *mokṣa*.

Let us turn next to the ways in which His *grace* (*karamu*) is said to work. So long as we go on enjoying good health, in spite of frequent dietic indulgence maybe, it is only occasionally that we may casually tend to regard our good health as a sign of His grace, in case we are religious at all. Yet, a quite unexpected bout of sickness too may in fact *be* an act of His grace if it impels us to grow self-critical, and so to isolate (and abstain from repeating) the misdemeanour we have been yielding to, *without our being able to look at the ailment in question explicitly as a quiet working of His grace*.

Take, again, the case of those who have been acclaimed as being truly religious. We see them working tirelessly for the sake of humanity and so we admire them specially. The Guru would however insist that it is His grace which enables these individuals to do all this good work, and to keep to the path of benevolence tirelessly, even in the face of misguided criticism occasionally. And, we may add, he is not alone in voicing this radical faith. Gandhi is just as categorical. See, here, his following personal testimony:

> We experience Him when, imperfect beings all, we are able to . . . tread the strait and narrow path (of righteous conduct) unfalteringly. That strength is from Him. It is Him.[49]

Further, again in our own day, whenever Mother Teresa was complimented on *her* having done such stupendous humanitarian work, did not her ready retort always run somewhat as follows: "No, nothing of the kind! It is *God*'s

---

[49] Pyarelal, *The Last Phase*, Navajivan, 1958, p. 475.

work. It had to succeed!"[50] And is it possible to assess the overall value of the work of these devout souls? No one would here say, *yes*. In other words, the working of His Grace, as it operates through such individuals of exalted spirituality, is for ever inestimable.

Be it noted, however, that being religious is not merely to believe that He is possessed of infinite attributes. One has to luxuriate in contemplating them; to deepen one's faith in their reality and power; and to attune one's life accordingly. This indeed is a part message of the 27th *pauḍī* which provides a rapturous account of the various ways in which, to the intensely devout Guru, elements of nature, saintly human beings, and gods and goddesses all look like celebrating the glory of God. For our purpose, however, the most helpful lines in this *pauḍī* run as follows:

> *soi soi sadā sachu sāhibu sāchā sāchī nāī* ।
> *hai bhī hosī jāi na jāsī rachnā jini rachāī* ।।[51]

We say so not merely because they affirm that God will continue to abide unaffected even when His creation comes to an end, but because its first two lines vindicate our interpretation of *satināmu* as: "His Name is Truth". (This *pauḍī* 27, we may note, appears again not only in *Rahirās*, the evening prayer, but also in *rāga āsā* on p. 347 of *Sri Guru Granth Sahib*.)

The shift from the 27th to the 28th *pauḍī* is to be noted with care. In the former we see the Guru's very being so attuned with God and His majesty that, quite without any effort on

---

[50] This is what Mother Teresa actually said during a television interview.

[51] *Japuji, pauḍī* 27.

his part, he is led not merely to think of, but to visualize very intensely the variform charms of Nature and devout souls as celebrating the glory of God. *Our* being, on the other hand, is not so attuned. We have to be exhorted and trained to prefer attitudes of ultimate, abiding value to what just works in daily life. In other words, *we* need *sādhnā*. Now, all *sādhnā* is discipline of the self by the self. Yet, in so far as He is the prime giver of all life[52] and capacity for endeavour, it is implicit dependence on His grace which can enable us not merely to make the requisite effort, but to improve it continually.

We may now take a collective yet admittedly imperfect look at three *pauḍīs* (27-29). Vinoba Bhave speaks of them as making a lovely lot.[53] This need not surprise us, for it suits his own devout temper perfectly. The trouble however is that he speaks of these *pauḍīs* as providing a very skilful composition from the poetic point of view and as designed in the way of a metaphor with *yoga* as its model (*pauḍī* 29). Now, this at once suggests some questions which Vinoba Bhave does not appear to envisage. Howsoever beautiful a metaphorical presentation may be, it never bares truth as it actually is, as against its mere semblance – that is, quite without some imaginative colouring. As strictly understood, a metaphor is an expression in which the person, action or thing referred to is described *as if* it really were what it merely resembles. Are we then to suppose that here the Guru is simply giving free rein to his imagination, as we also freely do in moments of vacancy. We too can resort to unfettered imagining and visualize gods and goddesses in our own ways. Yet there has to be some radical difference

---

52 *sabhnā jiā kā iku dātā so mai visari na jāī – Japuji, pauḍī* 5.

53 Vinoba Bhave, *Japuji*, p. 82.

between the Guru's envisioning and our own; and indeed there is. By and large, what we imagine does not convince us of its being real. It just remains a figment of the imagination. The Guru, on the other hand, just because of his intense devoutness and spiritual insight, *actually experiences – not merely imagines* – the various elements and features of creation as exulting in the glory of God; and we, as we are, have only to acquiesce in the truth and profundity of his transcendent vision. If a poet who, "in the hour of thoughtless youth"[54] has so far been fascinated only by the visual beauty of colour and form in the region of nature, suddenly intuits:

A presence that disturbs . . . with the joy
Of elevated thoughts; a sense sublime
Of something far more deeply interfused
. . .
A motion and a spirit, that impels
All thinking things, all objects of thought,
And rolls through all things. . . .[55]

are we to ignore this unusual experience as merely illusory?

Be it noted that a poet, a lover, and a devout person can all experience moments of utter surrender to the charm and significance of a chosen direction. We cannot dismiss such

---

54 These are Wordsworth's own words in his well-known poem "Tintern Abbey".

55 Ibid. William Wordsworths' poem composed a few miles above *Tintern Abbey* on revisiting the banks of the river Wye, during a tour, on 13 July 1798. Here, for accurate disposition of the words that make the quote, we are indebted to S.N. Prasad, Associate Professor (English), Hans Raj College, University of Delhi.

experience as unreal simply because it is not available to us in the run of everyday life. What indeed counts for the Guru is not merely the formal propriety of our *attitudes*, but the value and intensity of personal qualities and experience they may generate. This is why in this *pauḍī* (28) he prefers, as we would all expect, *genuine* inner humility to the mere desire to *appear* humble simply by moving around with *jholī*s and begging bowls; and true inner contentment with what one already has for a spartan living, as against the wooden *mudrā*s worn by some ascetics in their ears as ostentatious marks of austere living (*pauḍī* 28); and acquiscence in honest labour (plus abstinence) in opposition to servility or needless dependence on others.

With reference to people in general, as also with regard to those who explicitly try to cultivate goodness, we are told that (by and large) knowledge is had through the activity of our senses which are basically controlled by God; that, dominant – even obsessive – though *their* activity often is, *antarnād* or the voice of conscience, quite often unheeded, is never somnolent for long; that knowledge which nourishes us truly – and keeps us on the right track – results from His grace; and that whereas some of those who are enmeshed in worldliness try assiduously to acquire supernatural powers (*ṛddhi*s and *siddhi*s) for success in worldly affairs, the truly devout ones labour only for the supreme bliss of God-realization.

These, however, are not the only ways in which Guru Nanak speaks of God and the godly life. *Pauṛī*s 29 and 30 alike visualize God in some such uncommon ways as have not been treated at length by him earlier, and which call for some ancillary thinking by us. In *pauḍī* 29 God is said to be the source and supervisor of the regular, alternating changes which enable us to adjust our attitudes to life with a fair measure of confidence, such as the sequence of day and night, and of the seasons; or of confluence and separation (*saṁyoga* and *viyoga*), such as a son's launching into an independent career (we may say) after a number of restful years under the wings of his caring father. The next one (*pauḍī* 30) refers to God as *the One who sees us all*, but is Himself for ever quite unseen. Now, it is surely intriguing to speak of God in this uncommon way, but it is just not true to the Guru's *total* view of God. He says repeatedly that God's pervasive attitude towards us is one of love and benevolence. So the view that – though He oversees us all – God remains unseen Himself – has to be supplemented with the thought that He yet looks at us all surely not detachedly, but with *concern*, not in the sense of anxiety, but as sympathetic interest. The God that we love and worship cannot be a mere curio; and when our saints speak of Him as *samdarśi*, they only mean that He is equally concerned with everybody's welfare, though of course discriminatingly.

As for the *pauḍī* which follows (31), of all that it says the two following lines call for some careful thinking:

> *kari kari vekhai sirjaṇhāru* ।
> *nānak sache kī sāchī kār* ॥[56]

The literal meaning of the first line is clear. God goes on *looking at* what He creates. But what exactly is the way or the nature of this looking at? Does He look at what He creates in the way of a painter who is generally seen to go on *checking* what he has just done? We cannot say, *yes*; because whereas a painter's inspection may *at once be followed* by an attempt to cover the brush stroke that has been wrongly put with a better one, in respect of God's creativity there is clearly no

---

[56] *Japuji, pauḍī* 31.

question of anything going astray. So we may only say that whatever He creates remains entirely within His purview.

No such difficulty faces us at once as we turn to the second line. It says simply: because God, the creator, is Himself unfailingly true, His creation too cannot but be true. However, the moment we have said so, a question may well crop up. Has not the entire created world (*jagat*) often been dubbed as unreal (*mithyā*) by quite a few philosophers of religion? What then is the point in insisting that what He, the ultimate Real, creates must also be true? Luckily, some answer has here been provided by those whose life has not only been a mixture of good and evil, but who have also been a little thoughtful and even self-critical. Their verdict is balanced. They tell us that the world *becomes* a hotbed of evil when, in the obsessive pursuit of earthly ends, we forget Him totally and take to immoral ways; and that, contrarily, it remains quite *sat* or accordant with – or helpful to – the demands of truth if we all along bear in mind the requirements of a godly life.

Of the next two *pauḍī*s (32 and 33) only the second one calls for a good bit of reflection. The point of the first one is easy to see. It just provides yet another projection of the Guru's favourite emphasis that it is only by virtue of *His* grace that we can realize God; and that all other suggestions for attaining the same end are utterly vain:

nānak nadarī pāiai kūḍī kūḍai ṭhīs ।[57]

As for *pauḍī* 33, its basic ideas may be put as follows:

There is nothing human – no endeavour, attitude or achievement – on the basis of which we could determine,

---

[57] *Japuji, pauḍī* 32.

with perfect accuracy, our comparative goodness or lowliness as individuals. Only God can do so, because He alone knows how good or bad (on the whole) we really are. The world is often seen to lavish praise simply on the basis of the external results of our actions. Our motives, which may well be ignoble, often remain hidden and so unheeded. For us, therefore, the right attitude to adopt is simply to abstain from labelling some select individuals as good and others as bad. God alone has the power to do so:

> *jisu hathi joru kari vekhai soi* ।
> *nānak utamu nīchu na koi* ॥[58]

This, of course, is not to suggest that *we* do not have to try to become morally better. The Guru, in fact, projects five distinct disciplines or *khaṇḍ*s by following (or caring for) which we can grow in goodness, and so hope to be favoured with His grace – of course, if and when He condescends. But, as we turn to the five *khaṇḍ*s, and before we look at what their content or significance is, it seems needful to highlight the following general facts:

First, these *khaṇḍ*s make the closing – or rather the climactic – part of *Japuji*. So the interested reader – i.e. one who is really serious about making the most of this holy work in his own effort to cultivate devoutness – is expected to have paid close attention to all that comes earlier, particularly to the following major emphases of the Guru:

(a) A satisfying vision of God requires us to cultivate some essential qualities and attitudes, such as an abiding love for Him:

---

[58] *Japuji, pauḍī* 33.

viṇu guṇ kīte bhagati na hoi ।

. . .

sati suhāṇu sadā mani chāu ॥[59]

(b) How well we come to realize God depends entirely on His grace and benevolence:

jevaḍu āpi jāṇai āpi āpi ।
nānak nadarī karamī dāti ॥[60]

(c) It is surely God who grants liberation. But his greatest gift is to enliven one with the very impulse to love Him, because it is this primal stir of devoutness which can lead one to *mokṣa* ultimately:

jis no bakhse sifti sālāh ।
nānak pātisāhi pātisāhu ॥[61]

(d) It is only by virtue of His grace that we can realize God. All other suggestions for attaining the supreme end are vain:

nānak nadarī pāiai kūḍī kūḍai ṭhīs ॥[62]

(e) No one is good or lowly in himself. Only God has the power to make such judgements:

jisu hathi joru kari vekhai soi ।
nānak utamu nīchu na koi ॥[63]

Here, the first four citations (a–d) emphasize the love, grace and benevolence of God. The fifth one (e) requires us *not* to

---

[59] *Japuji, pauḍī* 21.

[60] Ibid., *pauḍī* 24.

[61] Ibid., *pauḍī* 25.

[62] Ibid., *pauḍī* 32.

[63] Ibid., *pauḍī* 33.

judge some men as morally superior to others, because (as already said) God alone (who knows even our hidden motives) has the power to do so. All these faiths and attitudes, we repeat, are expected to be already a part of the mental equipment of those who begin their moral ascent from the opening *dharam khaṇḍ*. What is more, the devotees are all supposed to have cultivated a genuine love of God, faith in His benevolence; *and to be eager to come ever closer to God.*

Second, without this prior equipment, we may say, the radical transition from *dharam khaṇḍ* (which is essentially an ethical stage) to *gyān khaṇḍ* which is a patently metaphysical state of experience, just cannot come about. To do duty as one's station in life demands is one thing; to have an overpowering (*prachaṇḍ*) vision of the entire universe is quite another. To obtain the latter one needs *divya dṛṣṭi*, like the one which was provided to Arjuna by Lord Kṛṣṇa on the battlefield. But this ethereal vision can come as a gesture of divine benevolence only when the devotee leaves himself entirely at His mercy.

It is (a) the cultivation of this specific faith that, in so far as we are all made of the same clay[64] – or are infected with identical weaknesses – no one may be adjudged as categorically inferior or superior to others; and (b) the collateral *catholicity* of attitude which (may together be said to) pave the way to *gyān khaṇḍ* with its astounding (*prachaṇḍ*) plenitude of multiple awareness, though surely not without the beneficence of His grace. *Dharam khaṇḍ* too, of course, has its own preparatory value for right living. One is here

64 *māti ek anek bhānti kari sāji sājanhārai – Sri Guru Granth Sahib*, p. 1350.

required to regulate actions and attitudes in accordance with the demands of varying situations faced in real life; and, in doing so, a sense of moral discrimination is very likely to emerge. Yet the overall concern *here* is mainly with the needs and demands of an individual life. The elevation to *gyān khaṇḍ*, on the other hand, is at once a dawn of limitless awareness. The Guru emphasizes both its extent and variform content. He does not, however, appear to visualize a question clearly which seems natural to us. Who are those select ones who get blessed with the passage to *gyān khaṇḍ*? The question is legitimate and cannot be ignored, for the lift from *dharam khaṇḍ* to *gyān khaṇḍ* cannot be automatic. Surely, not everyone whose daily conduct is fairly righteous can claim to have received the all-embracing vision which *gyān khaṇḍ* is said to provide. It may rather be said to be a gift of His grace only to those whom *He* has found to be truly virtuous, and who are yet ceaselessly engaged in the task of self-improvement (*śaram khaṇḍ*). But whatever be the process or reason of its being attained, once an individual finds himself in *gyān khaṇḍ* he gets blessed with a spectacle of (a) countless fields of action, as against his own limited, earthly one; (b) numberless stellar bodies and configurations with an overwhelming range of extent and variety; (c) saints and sages of various faiths; and (d) the running practice of multifarious methods of prayer and worship. What is more, the spectacle embraces a good many winds, waters and gods, all appearing to *regulate* whatever is there or comes to pass:

> *kete pavaṇ pāṇī vaisantar kete kān mahes* ।
> *kete barme ghāḍati ghaḍiahi rūp raṅg ke ves* ॥
> *ketiā karam bhūmī mer kete kete dhū updes* ।
> *kete ind chand sūr kete kete maṇḍal des* ॥
>
> . . .

. . . nānak antu na antu ||[65]

The *sādhnā* here, we may say, consists in adopting (what has been called) the attitude of wise passiveness; so, in just opening up to the vastness and variety of the universe; and therefore in getting even more deeply imbued with a sense of His infinite greatness and glory. What is more, the blessed individual here is not just the agent, nor even the mere bearer of the experience, but the very pulse of the revelation. Therefore, he brims over with joy and excitement at the experience of what has been revealed to him:

giān khaṇḍ mahi giānu parchaṇḍu |
tithai nād vinod koḍ anandu ||[66]

Thus invigorated, the individual in question gets engaged in the interminable process of attuning his being evermore – and of course single-mindedly – with what perfect devoutness demands:

saram khaṇḍ kī bāṇī rūpu |
tithai ghāḍati ghaḍiai bahutu anūpu ||
. . .
tithai ghaḍiai surā sidhā ki sudhi ||[67]

The next *pauḍī* (37), which speaks of the two higher *khaṇḍ*s, is really a two-in-one. It may well be said to visualize two adjacent shades of the devotee–deity relation, the state of

65 *Japuji, pauḍī* 35.

66 Ibid., *pauḍī* 36. Incidentally, this also explains why Guru Nanak's own utterances are, as a rule, impassioned and ornate, though they do not anywhere show lack of relevance or significance.

67 *Japuji, pauḍī* 36.

communion tending to elevate into one of unruffled absorption of the devotee's identity in God-consciousness. Take, to begin with, the first ten lines (*karam khaṇḍ – sachā mani soi*). Here, the Guru speaks of *luminaries* in the realm of *sādhnā* (*mahā bal sūr*) – i.e. of those who are (or have been) thoroughly imbued with the love of God (Rāma) and His glory (Sītā *mahimā*) – and (so also) of their perennial luxuriating in bliss:

> *karahi anandu sachā mani soi* ।[68]

Then, from the eleventh line onward, all that is said relates to the realm of absolute Truth where *niraṅkār* (or *nirākār*) alone abides; and where, having created the world, He just keeps looking at and blessing it:

> *sach khaṇḍi vasai niraṅkāru* ।
> *kari kari vekhai nadari nihāl* ।।[69]

Here, in the climactic fifth (i.e. *such*) *khaṇḍ*, God alone is said to abide, and the *sādhak*, we may say, has lost his identity completely – and, of course, wilfully and very happily – in unruffled experience of divinity. The placement of these two *khaṇḍ*s in the same *pauḍī* need not appear odd. Varying absorption in the object of attention is quite a common experience. What faces us at any moment may either be sought to be understood (more or less objectively) or just allowed to capture us as an influence. In the course of devout

---

68 Ibid., *pauḍī* 37.

69 Ibid. By and large, however, what has been found indispensable is the pursuit of a course of multiple self-discipline which the next *pauḍī* (38) crystallizes penetratively, if by way of a metaphor.

living, however, the *bhakta*'s disposition in relation to God is neither so simple nor so automatic. Whether it is done as a yearning for release from engulfment in carnal pleasures, or as a paean of praise and gratitude for enabling one to face and overcome a desperate situation in daily life, what is always needed for praying is some ideal space for communing with God. On the other hand, the bliss which a devotee experiences in getting closer to God in deepening faith is very likely to make him pine for absolute oneness with Him in self-effacing love. In our country both kinds of devotees have all along illumined the firmament of *bhakti*.

To turn now to the *pauḍī* 38, we find it quintessential in significance, and this as follows:

(a) It provides a succinct account of the manifold discipline which alone can enable one not only to experience that crowning blessedness that goes with the consummate experience of His (look of) grace, but also to feel edified enough to recite His Name with the requisite measure of devoutness, whereupon the individual in question may be said to have become a veritable mint (or *ṭaksāl*) for coining words of divine wisdom.

(b) By emphasizing the complexity and rigour of the discipline in question, this *pauḍī* may be expected to counter a possible misunderstanding to which casual readers can easily succumb in attending to some of the readily appealing utterances that come well before this *pauḍī*. For instance, by virtue of the very felicity of its run, the following couplet is likely to create the (mistaken) impression that getting committed to the Name – and ensuring total felicity for oneself – is a kind of easy give and take:

gāviai suṇiai mani rakhiai bhāu ।
dukhu parhari sukhu ghari lai jāi ॥[70]

What is more, the impression in question can easily intensify if, as is quite likely, in focusing on the thought that unfailing love and benevolence distinguish the very nature of God:

sāchā sāhibu sāchu nāi bhākhiā bhāu apāru ।
ākhahi mangahi dehi dehi dāti kare dātāru ॥[71]

we become complacent in respect of *our own eligibility* for His grace. It is such facileness of thought and attitude which is set at nought by a careful look at what this *pauḍī* (38) formulates (and recommends) as the essential, but rigorous and intricate discipline for realizing the true significance of the Name. It may also be taken to counter a glib, yet quite probable misinterpretation of lines such as the following:

mani jītai jagu jītu;

and the point here is easy to bring out. In everyday life whenever we talk about (or recommend) the self-control which words like *man jītnā* or *man mārnā* imply, the reference generally is to some *specific* craving or obsession which has to be checked from prevailing – in a *particular* situation. But here (in *pauḍī* 28) what the words *mani jītai jagu jītu* really signify is that *pervasive and abiding self-control* which crowns the successful practice of the multiple, *rigorous* – and possibly lifelong – self-discipline which *pauḍī* 38 formulates and enjoins.

---

70 *Japuji, pauḍī* 5.

71 Ibid., *pauḍī* 4.

In this *pauḍī*, we may note, the very metaphor of a goldsmith *hammering* a piece of metal to the requisite degree of fineness *in the raging fire of a furnace* suggests that the discipline envisaged (and recommended) is a fiery ordeal (which, we may add, cannot be weathered without His grace).[72] The rigour of the entire discipline is borne out further by a careful look at its individual steps. Thus, to begin with the very first of these – i.e. continence or control over one's natural appetites and passions – it can never be an instant accomplishment; and the reason is easy to see. As actually experienced, none of our psycho-physical urges is a static stretch. They are all intermittent, and therefore call for *recurrent*, and immediate attention and control. This justifies the metaphor of repeated hammer*ing* – say, as against the use of a single, overpowering sledgehammer blow. Abiding and impeccable self-control can never be achieved at once. However earnest and watchful be our attempt to practise it, we are bound to falter now and then. We have to keep checking where and why we tend to fail. The need here is to exercise what has been called *ahrani* (intelligence, discrimination) in the *pauḍī* we are dealing with.

All this, however, relates only to how we are to behave positively. The negative aspect of the practice of self-discipline is yet to be emphasized. We have to abstain from trespasses into wrong conduct, be they intentional or inadvertent. Here, we are helped (in part) by the fear of

---

72 Be it noted, here, that Guru Nanak is not alone in using the metaphor of a furnace. Thus, see the following:

"Our prayers should be burning words coming forth from the *furnace* of hearts filled with love" — Mother Teresa, *Everything Starts From Prayer: A Full Circle Book*, 2nd reprint, June 2007, p. 72

God regarded as the One whose eye misses nothing. This is *bhāu*. This mere fear, however, cannot carry us through. To bear the rigour of the total discipline, and to abstain from wrong conduct maximally, we have to turn to His help recurrently, with the fatih that it is His very nature to love us and to care for our welfare. In other words, we have not merely to fear and revere God but to love Him as well.

It is only when our being has *thus* become suitably oriented – i.e. through meticulous and uncompromising self-discipline, nourished all along by a *reverent* love of God – that it can serve as the proper *bhāṇḍā* (receptacle) for the nectar of His Name. In other words, it is only then that the *sādhak* can:

(a) recite His (immortalizing) Name with the requisite measure of purity and devoutness:

bhāṇḍā bhāu amr̥tu titu ḍhāli;[73]

(b) give utterance to words of impeccable truth and wisdom:

ghaḍīai sabadu sachī ṭaksāl;[74] and

(c) also feel overwhelmingly blessed with His (look of) grace:

nānak nadarī nadari nihāl.[75]

It is precisely some such select individuals who are spoken of admiringly in the *Saloku* which follows and with which *Japuji* may be said to *culminate.*

---

73 *Japuji, pauḍī* 38.

74 Ibid.

75 Ibid.

Saloku

INDEED, this composition, *Saloku,* consummates *Japuji.* We speak thus advisedly. *Saloku* is no ordinary ending. With one stroke of the brush, as it were, the composer (Guru Aṅgad Dev)[76] here distinguishes what *God* provides for the normal run of human life from how *we* avail of it all – routinely, often casually; and, finally, from how it can be, and has been used ideally. Literally, this succinct but intense piece runs (more or less) as follows.

God has provided all the essentials that life needs for its uninterrupted run – namely, air, water, fire, earth; and the cycle of day and night. Of all these, the air that we breathe may be said to be primary or *guru.*[77] Without breathing we cannot live even for a moment. However, for the everyday conduct of life, and to meet the demands it makes on our body, the day–night cycle is also indispensable. It provides for both activity and recuperation of energy, and so may be said to nourish us like our parents. What is more, this set-up of God-given facilities is by no means temporary. By and large, it abides. *We* alone waver in respect of how we avail of it, i.e. in respect of the quality of our everyday conduct;

---

76 As is well known, *Saloku* is a composition of Guru Aṅgad Dev. But it is so clearly in tune with the spirit of Guru Nanak's views that it is common practice to regard it as the end-part of *Japuji* itself.

77 Air is clearly the primary condition of life, and has therefore been called *guru,* that is, pre-eminent. It is, in this context, noteworthy that in *dharam khaṇḍ,* where the Guru quickly lists the essentials of life, *pavaṇ* is made to head the list. There, the second line runs thus – *kete pavaṇ pāṇī baisantar kete kān mahes.*

are judged as good or bad by God's impeccable wisdom; so remain more or less away from Him; and therefore subject to adversity in varying degree. On the other hand, those devotees whose life has been one of steadfast commitment to the Name, transcend the very possibility of pain and suffering; and their faces come to acquire a glow which bespeaks consummate self-discipline and the bliss of having realized their spiritual destiny. What is more, quite a few other individuals have gained spiritually from the example and company of these blessed ones.

Thus, whereas it opens as an essentially transcendent invocation to God, *Japuji* ends with a celebration, so to say, of some rare human beings of consummate godliness. The work admittedly abounds in esoteric thoughts and images, but this is just as clear that its main purpose is patently humane. This is what makes it a powerful vehicle of the values that lend to human life its distinctive glory and significance.

Japu Ji
Text (Trilingual)

ੴ

ਸਤਿ ਨਾਮੁ ਕਰਤਾ ਪੁਰਖੁ ਨਿਰਭਉ ਨਿਰਵੈਰੁ
ਅਕਾਲ ਮੂਰਤਿ ਅਜੂਨੀ ਸੈਭੰ ਗੁਰ ਪ੍ਰਸਾਦਿ ॥

१ ओंकार

सति नामु करता पुरखु निरभउ निरवैरु
अकाल मूरति अजूनी सैभं गुर प्रसादि ॥

Ek Oṁkār

sati nāmu kartā purakhu nirbhau nirvairu
akāl mūrati ajūnī saibhaṁ gur prasādi ॥

॥ ਜਪੁ ॥

ਸਲੋਕੁ

ਆਦਿ ਸਚੁ ਜੁਗਾਦਿ ਸਚੁ ॥

ਹੈ ਭੀ ਸਚੁ ਨਾਨਕ ਹੋਸੀ ਭੀ ਸਚੁ ॥੧॥

॥ जपु ॥

सलोकु

आदि सचु जुगादि सचु ॥

है भी सचु नानक होसी भी सचु ॥१॥

|| **Japu** ||

Saloku

ādi sachu jugādi sachu ||

hai bhī sachu nānak hosī bhī sachu ||1||

ਸੋਚੈ ਸੋਚਿ ਨ ਹੋਵਈ ਜੇ ਸੋਚੀ ਲਖ ਵਾਰ ॥
ਚੁਪੈ ਚੁਪ ਨ ਹੋਵਈ ਜੇ ਲਾਇ ਰਹਾ ਲਿਵ ਤਾਰ ॥
ਭੁਖਿਆ ਭੁਖ ਨ ਉਤਰੀ ਜੇ ਬੰਨਾ ਪੁਰੀਆ ਭਾਰ ॥
ਸਹਸ ਸਿਆਣਪਾ ਲਖ ਹੋਹਿ ਤ ਇਕ ਨ ਚਲੈ ਨਾਲਿ ॥
ਕਿਵ ਸਚਿਆਰਾ ਹੋਈਐ ਕਿਵ ਕੂੜੈ ਤੁਟੈ ਪਾਲਿ ॥
ਹੁਕਮਿ ਰਜਾਈ ਚਲਣਾ ਨਾਨਕ ਲਿਖਿਆ ਨਾਲਿ ॥੧॥

सोचै सोचि न होवई जे सोची लख वार ॥
चुपै चुप न होवई जे लाइ रहा लिव तार ॥
भुखिआ भुख न उतरी जे बन्ना पुरीआ भार ॥
सहस सिआणपा लख होहि त इक न चलै नालि ॥
किव सचिआरा होईऐ किव कूड़ै तुटै पालि ॥
हुकमि रजाई चलणा नानक लिखिआ नालि ॥१॥

sochai sochi na hovaī je sochī lakh vār ॥
chupai chup na hovaī je lāi rahā liv tār ॥
bhukhiā bhukh na utrī je bannā puriā bhār ॥
sahas siāṇpā lakh hohi ta ik na chalai nāli ॥
kiv sachiārā hoīai kiv kūḍai tuṭai pāli ॥
hukmi rajāī chalṇā nānak likhiā nāli ॥1॥

ਹੁਕਮੀ ਹੋਵਨਿ ਆਕਾਰ ਹੁਕਮੁ ਨ ਕਹਿਆ ਜਾਈ ॥
ਹੁਕਮੀ ਹੋਵਨਿ ਜੀਅ ਹੁਕਮਿ ਮਿਲੈ ਵਡਿਆਈ ॥
ਹੁਕਮੀ ਉਤਮੁ ਨੀਚੁ ਹੁਕਮਿ ਲਿਖਿ ਦੁਖ ਸੁਖ ਪਾਈਅਹਿ ॥
ਇਕਨਾ ਹੁਕਮੀ ਬਖਸੀਸ ਇਕਿ ਹੁਕਮੀ ਸਦਾ ਭਵਾਈਅਹਿ ॥
ਹੁਕਮੈ ਅੰਦਰਿ ਸਭੁ ਕੋ ਬਾਹਰਿ ਹੁਕਮ ਨ ਕੋਇ ॥
ਨਾਨਕ ਹੁਕਮੈ ਜੇ ਬੁਝੈ ਤ ਹਉਮੈ ਕਹੈ ਨ ਕੋਇ ॥੨॥

हुकमी होवनि आकार हुकमु न कहिआ जाई ॥
हुकमी होवनि जीअ हुकमि मिलै वडिआई ॥
हुकमी उतमु नीचु हुकमि लिखि दुख सुख पाईअहि ॥
इकना हुकमी बखसीस इकि हुकमी सदा भवाईअहि ॥
हुकमै अंदरि सभु को बाहरि हुकम न कोइ ॥
नानक हुकमै जे बुझै त हउमै कहै न कोइ ॥२॥

hukmī hovani ākār hukmu na kahiā jāī ॥
hukmī hovani jīa hukmi milai vaḍiāī ॥
hukmī utamu nīchu hukmi likhi dukh sukh pāīahi ॥
iknā hukmī bakhsīs iki hukmī sadā bhavāīahi ॥
hukmai andari sabhu ko bāhari hukm na koi ॥
nānak hukmai je bujhai ta haumai kahai na koi ॥2॥

ਗਾਵੈ ਕੋ ਤਾਣੁ ਹੋਵੈ ਕਿਸੈ ਤਾਣੁ ॥
ਗਾਵੈ ਕੋ ਦਾਤਿ ਜਾਣੈ ਨੀਸਾਣੁ ॥
ਗਾਵੈ ਕੋ ਗੁਣ ਵਡਿਆਈਆ ਚਾਰ ॥
ਗਾਵੈ ਕੋ ਵਿਦਿਆ ਵਿਖਮੁ ਵੀਚਾਰੁ ॥
ਗਾਵੈ ਕੋ ਸਾਜਿ ਕਰੇ ਤਨੁ ਖੇਹ ॥
ਗਾਵੈ ਕੋ ਜੀਅ ਲੈ ਫਿਰਿ ਦੇਹ ॥
ਗਾਵੈ ਕੋ ਜਾਪੈ ਦਿਸੈ ਦੂਰਿ ॥

गावै को ताणु होवै किसै ताणु ॥
गावै को दाति जाणै नीसाणु ॥
गावै को गुण वडिआईआ चार ॥
गावै को विदिआ विखमु वीचारु ॥
गावै को साजि करे तनु खेह ॥
गावै को जीअ लै फिरि देह ॥
गावै को जापै दिसै दूरि ॥

gāvai ko tāṇu hovai kisai tāṇu ॥
gāvai ko dāti jāṇai nīsāṇu ॥
gāvai ko guṇ vaḍiāīā chār ॥
gāvai ko vidiā vikhamu vīchāru ॥
gāvai ko sāji kare tanu kheh ॥
gāvai ko jīa lai phiri deh ॥
gāvai ko jāpai disai dūri ॥

ਗਾਵੈ ਕੋ ਵੇਖੈ ਹਾਦਰਾ ਹਦੂਰਿ ॥
ਕਥਨਾ ਕਥੀ ਨ ਆਵੈ ਤੋਟਿ ॥
ਕਥਿ ਕਥਿ ਕਥੀ ਕੋਟੀ ਕੋਟਿ ਕੋਟਿ ॥
ਦੇਦਾ ਦੇ ਲੈਦੇ ਥਕਿ ਪਾਹਿ ॥
ਜੁਗਾ ਜੁਗੰਤਰਿ ਖਾਹੀ ਖਾਹਿ ॥
ਹੁਕਮੀ ਹੁਕਮੁ ਚਲਾਏ ਰਾਹੁ ॥
ਨਾਨਕ ਵਿਗਸੈ ਵੇਪਰਵਾਹੁ ॥੩॥

गावै को वेखै हादरा हदूरि ॥
कथना कथी न आवै तोटि ॥
कथि कथि कथी कोटी कोटि कोटि ॥
देदा दे लैदे थकि पाहि ॥
जुगा जुगंतरि खाही खाहि ॥
हुकमी हुकमु चलाए राहु ॥
नानक विगसै वेपरवाहु ॥३॥

gāvai ko vekhai hādrā hadūri ॥
kathnā kathī na āvai toṭi ॥
kathi kathi kathī koṭī koṭi koṭi ॥
dedā de laide thaki pāhi ॥
jugā jugantari khāhī khāhi ॥
hukmī hukmu chalāe rāhu ॥
nānak vigsai veparvāhu ॥3॥

ਸਾਚਾ ਸਾਹਿਬੁ ਸਾਚੁ ਨਾਇ ਭਾਖਿਆ ਭਾਉ ਅਪਾਰੁ ॥
ਆਖਹਿ ਮੰਗਹਿ ਦੇਹਿ ਦੇਹਿ ਦਾਤਿ ਕਰੇ ਦਾਤਾਰੁ ॥
ਫੇਰਿ ਕਿ ਅਗੈ ਰਖੀਐ ਜਿਤੁ ਦਿਸੈ ਦਰਬਾਰੁ ॥
ਮੁਹੌ ਕਿ ਬੋਲਣੁ ਬੋਲੀਐ ਜਿਤੁ ਸੁਣਿ ਧਰੇ ਪਿਆਰੁ ॥
ਅੰਮ੍ਰਿਤ ਵੇਲਾ ਸਚੁ ਨਾਉ ਵਡਿਆਈ ਵੀਚਾਰੁ ॥
ਕਰਮੀ ਆਵੈ ਕਪੜਾ ਨਦਰੀ ਮੋਖੁ ਦੁਆਰੁ ॥
ਨਾਨਕ ਏਵੈ ਜਾਣੀਐ ਸਭੁ ਆਪੇ ਸਚਿਆਰੁ ॥੪॥

साचा साहिबु साचु नाइ भाखिआ भाउ अपारु ॥
आखहि मंगहि देहि देहि दाति करे दातारु ॥
फेरि कि अगै रखीऐ जितु दिसै दरबारु ॥
मुहौ कि बोलणु बोलीऐ जितु सुणि धरे पिआरु ॥
अमृत वेला सचु नाउ वडिआई वीचारु ॥
करमी आवै कपड़ा नदरी मोखु दुआरु ॥
नानक एवै जाणीऐ सभु आपे सचिआरु ॥४॥

sāchā sāhibu sāchu nāi bhākhiā bhāu apāru ॥
ākhahi mangahi dehi dehi dāti kare dātāru ॥
pheri ki agai rakhīai jitu disai darbāru ॥
muhau ki bolaṇu bolīai jitu suṇi dhare piāru ॥
amṛt velā sachu nāu vaḍiāī vīchāru ॥
karamī āvai kapḍā nadarī mokhu duāru ॥
nānak evai jāṇīai sabhu āpe sachiāru ॥4॥

ਥਾਪਿਆ ਨ ਜਾਇ ਕੀਤਾ ਨ ਹੋਇ ॥
ਆਪੇ ਆਪਿ ਨਿਰੰਜਨੁ ਸੋਇ ॥
ਜਿਨਿ ਸੇਵਿਆ ਤਿਨਿ ਪਾਇਆ ਮਾਨੁ ॥
ਨਾਨਕ ਗਾਵੀਐ ਗੁਣੀ ਨਿਧਾਨੁ ॥
ਗਾਵੀਐ ਸੁਣੀਐ ਮਨਿ ਰਖੀਐ ਭਾਉ ॥
ਦੁਖੁ ਪਰਹਰਿ ਸੁਖੁ ਘਰਿ ਲੈ ਜਾਇ ॥
ਗੁਰਮੁਖਿ ਨਾਦੰ ਗੁਰਮੁਖਿ ਵੇਦੰ ਗੁਰਮੁਖਿ ਰਹਿਆ ਸਮਾਈ ॥
ਗੁਰੁ ਈਸਰੁ ਗੁਰੁ ਗੋਰਖੁ ਬਰਮਾ ਗੁਰੁ ਪਾਰਬਤੀ ਮਾਈ ॥
ਜੇ ਹਉ ਜਾਣਾ ਆਖਾ ਨਾਹੀ ਕਹਣਾ ਕਥਨੁ ਨ ਜਾਈ ॥
ਗੁਰਾ ਇਕ ਦੇਹਿ ਬੁਝਾਈ ॥
ਸਭਨਾ ਜੀਆ ਕਾ ਇਕੁ ਦਾਤਾ ਸੋ ਮੈ ਵਿਸਰਿ ਨ ਜਾਈ ॥੫॥

थापिआ न जाइ कीता न होइ ॥
आपे आपि निरंजनु सोइ ॥
जिनि सेविआ तिनि पाइआ मानु ॥
नानक गावीऐ गुणी निधानु ॥
गावीऐ सुणीऐ मनि रखीऐ भाउ ॥
दुखु परहरि सुखु घरि लै जाइ ॥
गुरमुखि नादं गुरमुखि वेदं गुरमुखि रहिआ समाई ॥
गुरु ईसरु गुरु गोरखु बरमा गुरु पारबती माई ॥
जे हउ जाणा आखा नाही कहणा कथनु न जाई ॥
गुरा इक देहि बुझाई ॥
सभना जीआ का इकु दाता सो मै विसरि न जाई ॥५॥

thāpiā na jāi kītā na hoi ||
āpe āpi nirañjanu soi ||
jini seviā tini pāiā mānu ||
nānak gāvīai guṇī nidhānu ||
gāvīai suṇīai mani rakhīai bhāu ||
dukhu parhari sukhu ghari lai jāi ||
gurmukhi nādaṁ gurmukhi vedaṁ gurmukhi rahiā samāī ||
guru īsaru guru gorakhu barmā guru pārbatī māī ||
je hau jāṇā ākhā nāhī kahṇā kathanu na jāī ||
gurā ik dehi bujhāī ||
sabhnā jīā kā iku dātā so mai visari na jāī ||5||

ਤੀਰਥਿ ਨਾਵਾ ਜੇ ਤਿਸੁ ਭਾਵਾ ਵਿਣੁ ਭਾਣੇ ਕਿ ਨਾਇ ਕਰੀ ॥
ਜੇਤੀ ਸਿਰਠਿ ਉਪਾਈ ਵੇਖਾ ਵਿਣੁ ਕਰਮਾ ਕਿ ਮਿਲੈ ਲਈ ॥
ਮਤਿ ਵਿਚਿ ਰਤਨ ਜਵਾਹਰ ਮਾਣਿਕ ਜੇ ਇਕ ਗੁਰ ਕੀ ਸਿਖ ਸੁਣੀ ॥
ਗੁਰਾ ਇਕ ਦੇਹਿ ਬੁਝਾਈ ॥
ਸਭਨਾ ਜੀਆ ਕਾ ਇਕੁ ਦਾਤਾ ਸੋ ਮੈ ਵਿਸਰਿ ਨ ਜਾਈ ॥੬॥

तीरथि नावा जे तिसु भावा विणु भाणे कि नाइ करी ॥
जेती सिरठि उपाई वेखा विणु करमा कि मिलै लई ॥
मति विचि रतन जवाहर माणिक जे इक गुर की सिख सुणी ॥
गुरा इक देहि बुझाई ॥
सभना जीआ का इकु दाता सो मै विसरि न जाई ॥६॥

tīrathi nāvā je tisu bhāvā viṇu bhāṇe ki nāi karī ॥
jetī siraṭhi upāī vekhā viṇu karmā ki milai laī ॥
mati vichi ratan javāhar māṇik je ik gur kī sikh suṇī ॥
gurā ik dehi bujhāī ॥
sabhnā jīā kā iku dātā so mai visari na jāī ॥6॥

ਜੇ ਜੁਗ ਚਾਰੇ ਆਰਜਾ ਹੋਰ ਦਸੂਣੀ ਹੋਇ ॥
ਨਵਾ ਖੰਡਾ ਵਿਚਿ ਜਾਣੀਐ ਨਾਲਿ ਚਲੈ ਸਭੁ ਕੋਇ ॥
ਚੰਗਾ ਨਾਉ ਰਖਾਇ ਕੈ ਜਸੁ ਕੀਰਤਿ ਜਗਿ ਲੇਇ ॥
ਜੇ ਤਿਸੁ ਨਦਰਿ ਨ ਆਵਈ ਤ ਵਾਤ ਨ ਪੁਛੈ ਕੇ ॥
ਕੀਟਾ ਅੰਦਰਿ ਕੀਟੁ ਕਰਿ ਦੋਸੀ ਦੋਸੁ ਧਰੇ ॥
ਨਾਨਕ ਨਿਰਗੁਣਿ ਗੁਣੁ ਕਰੇ ਗੁਣਵੰਤਿਆ ਗੁਣੁ ਦੇ ॥
ਤੇਹਾ ਕੋਇ ਨ ਸੁਝਈ ਜਿ ਤਿਸੁ ਗੁਣੁ ਕੋਇ ਕਰੇ ॥੭॥

जे जुग चारे आरजा होर दसूणी होइ ॥
नवा खंडा विचि जाणीऐ नालि चलै सभु कोइ ॥
चंगा नाउ रखाइ कै जसु कीरति जगि लेइ ॥
जे तिसु नदरि न आवई त वात न पुछै के ॥
कीटा अंदरि कीटु करि दोसी दोसु धरे ॥
नानक निरगुणि गुणु करे गुणवंतिआ गुणु दे ॥
तेहा कोइ न सुझई जि तिसु गुणु कोइ करे ॥७॥

je jug chāre ārajā hor dasūṇī hoi ॥
navā khaṇḍā vichi jāṇīai nāli chalai sabhu koi ॥
changā nāu rakhāi kai jasu kīrati jagi lei ॥
je tisu nadari na āvaī ta vāt na puchhai ke ॥
kīṭā andari kīṭu kari dosī dosu dhare ॥
nānak nirguṇi guṇu kare guṇvantiā guṇu de ॥
tehā koi na sujhaī ji tisu guṇu koi kare ॥7॥

ਸੁਣਿਐ ਸਿਧ ਪੀਰ ਸੁਰਿ ਨਾਥ ॥
ਸੁਣਿਐ ਧਰਤਿ ਧਵਲ ਆਕਾਸ ॥
ਸੁਣਿਐ ਦੀਪ ਲੋਅ ਪਾਤਾਲ ॥
ਸੁਣਿਐ ਪੋਹਿ ਨ ਸਕੈ ਕਾਲੁ ॥
ਨਾਨਕ ਭਗਤਾ ਸਦਾ ਵਿਗਾਸੁ ॥
ਸੁਣਿਐ ਦੂਖ ਪਾਪ ਕਾ ਨਾਸੁ ॥੮॥

सुणिऐ सिध पीर सुरि नाथ ॥
सुणिऐ धरति धवल आकास ॥
सुणिऐ दीप लोअ पाताल ॥
सुणिऐ पोहि न सकै कालु ॥
नानक भगता सदा विगासु ॥
सुणिऐ दूख पाप का नासु ॥८॥

suṇiai sidh pīr suri nāth ॥
suṇiai dharati dhaval ākās ॥
suṇiai dīp loa pātāl ॥
suṇiai pohi na sakai kālu ॥
nānak bhagtā sadā vigāsu ॥
suṇiai dūkh pāp kā nāsu ॥8॥

ਸੁਣਿਐ ਈਸਰੁ ਬਰਮਾ ਇੰਦੁ ॥
ਸੁਣਿਐ ਮੁਖਿ ਸਾਲਾਹਣ ਮੰਦੁ ॥
ਸੁਣਿਐ ਜੋਗ ਜੁਗਤਿ ਤਨਿ ਭੇਦ ॥
ਸੁਣਿਐ ਸਾਸਤ ਸਿਮ੍ਰਿਤਿ ਵੇਦ ॥
ਨਾਨਕ ਭਗਤਾ ਸਦਾ ਵਿਗਾਸੁ ॥
ਸੁਣਿਐ ਦੂਖ ਪਾਪ ਕਾ ਨਾਸੁ ॥੯॥

सुणिऐ ईसरु बरमा इंदु ॥
सुणिऐ मुखि सालाहण मंदु ॥
सुणिऐ जोग जुगति तनि भेद ॥
सुणिऐ सासत सिमृति वेद ॥
नानक भगता सदा विगासु ॥
सुणिऐ दूख पाप का नासु ॥९॥

suṇiai īsaru barmā indu ॥
suṇiai mukhi sālāhaṇ mandu ॥
suṇiai jog jugati tani bhed ॥
suṇiai sāsat simr̥ti ved ॥
nānak bhagtā sadā vigāsu ॥
suṇiai dūkh pāp kā nāsu ॥9॥

ਸੁਣਿਐ ਸਤੁ ਸੰਤੋਖੁ ਗਿਆਨੁ ॥
ਸੁਣਿਐ ਅਠਸਠਿ ਕਾ ਇਸਨਾਨੁ ॥
ਸੁਣਿਐ ਪੜਿ ਪੜਿ ਪਾਵਹਿ ਮਾਨੁ ॥
ਸੁਣਿਐ ਲਾਗੈ ਸਹਜਿ ਧਿਆਨੁ ॥
ਨਾਨਕ ਭਗਤਾ ਸਦਾ ਵਿਗਾਸੁ ॥
ਸੁਣਿਐ ਦੂਖ ਪਾਪ ਕਾ ਨਾਸੁ ॥੧੦॥

सुणिऐ सतु संतोखु गिआनु ॥
सुणिऐ अठसठि का इसनानु ॥
सुणिऐ पड़ि पड़ि पावहि मानु ॥
सुणिऐ लागै सहजि धिआनु ॥
नानक भगता सदा विगासु ॥
सुणिऐ दूख पाप का नासु ॥१०॥

suṇiai satu santokhu giānu॥
suṇiai aṭhsaṭhi kā isnānu ॥
suṇiai paḍi paḍi pāvahi mānu ॥
suṇiai lāgai sahaji dhiānu ॥
nānak bhagtā sadā vigāsu ॥
suṇiai dūkh pāp kā nāsu ॥10॥

ਸੁਣਿਐ ਸਰਾ ਗੁਣਾ ਕੇ ਗਾਹ ॥
ਸੁਣਿਐ ਸੇਖ ਪੀਰ ਪਾਤਿਸਾਹ ॥
ਸੁਣਿਐ ਅੰਧੇ ਪਾਵਹਿ ਰਾਹੁ ॥
ਸੁਣਿਐ ਹਾਥ ਹੋਵੈ ਅਸਗਾਹੁ ॥
ਨਾਨਕ ਭਗਤਾ ਸਦਾ ਵਿਗਾਸੁ ॥
ਸੁਣਿਐ ਦੂਖ ਪਾਪ ਕਾ ਨਾਸੁ ॥੧੧॥

सुणिऐ सरा गुणा के गाह ॥
सुणिऐ सेख पीर पातिसाह ॥
सुणिऐ अंधे पावहि राहु ॥
सुणिऐ हाथ होवै असगाहु ॥
नानक भगता सदा विगासु ॥
सुणिऐ दूख पाप का नासु ॥११॥

suṇiai sarā guṇā ke gāh ॥
suṇiai sekh pīr pātisāh ॥
suṇiai andhe pāvahi rāhu ॥
suṇiai hāth hovai asgāhu ॥
nānak bhagtā sadā vigāsu ॥
suṇiai dūkh pāp kā nāsu ॥11॥

ਮੰਨੇ ਕੀ ਗਤਿ ਕਹੀ ਨ ਜਾਇ ॥
ਜੇ ਕੋ ਕਹੈ ਪਿਛੈ ਪਛੁਤਾਇ ॥
ਕਾਗਦਿ ਕਲਮ ਨ ਲਿਖਣਹਾਰੁ ॥
ਮੰਨੇ ਕਾ ਬਹਿ ਕਰਨਿ ਵੀਚਾਰੁ ॥
ਐਸਾ ਨਾਮੁ ਨਿਰੰਜਨੁ ਹੋਇ ॥
ਜੇ ਕੋ ਮੰਨਿ ਜਾਣੈ ਮਨਿ ਕੋਇ ॥੧੨॥

मंनै की गति कही न जाइ ॥
जे को कहै पिछै पछुताइ ॥
कागदि कलम न लिखणहारु ॥
मंनै का बहि करनि वीचारु ॥
ऐसा नामु निरंजनु होइ ॥
जे को मंनि जाणै मनि कोइ ॥१२॥

mannai kī gati kahī na jāi ॥
je ko kahai pichhai pachhutāi ॥
kāgadi kalam na likhaṇhāru ॥
mannai kā bahi karni vīchāru ॥
aisā nāmu nirañjanu hoi ॥
je ko manni jāṇai mani koi ॥12॥

ਮੰਨੈ ਸੁਰਤਿ ਹੋਵੈ ਮਨਿ ਬੁਧਿ ॥
ਮੰਨੈ ਸਗਲ ਭਵਣ ਕੀ ਸੁਧਿ ॥
ਮੰਨੈ ਮੁਹਿ ਚੋਟਾ ਨਾ ਖਾਇ ॥
ਮੰਨੈ ਜਮ ਕੈ ਸਾਥਿ ਨ ਜਾਇ ॥
ਐਸਾ ਨਾਮੁ ਨਿਰੰਜਨੁ ਹੋਇ ॥
ਜੇ ਕੋ ਮੰਨਿ ਜਾਣੈ ਮਨਿ ਕੋਇ ॥੧੩॥

मंनै सुरति होवै मनि बुधि ॥
मंनै सगल भवण की सुधि ॥
मंनै मुहि चोटा ना खाइ ॥
मंनै जम कै साथि न जाइ ॥
ऐसा नामु निरंजनु होइ ॥
जे को मंनि जाणै मनि कोइ ॥१३॥

mannai surati hovai mani budhi ॥
mannai sagal bhavaṇ kī sudhi ॥
mannai muhi choṭā nā khāi ॥
mannai jam kai sāthi na jāi ॥
aisā nāmu nirañjanu hoi ॥
je ko manni jāṇai mani koi ॥13॥

ਮੰਨੈ ਮਾਰਗਿ ਠਾਕ ਨ ਪਾਇ ॥
ਮੰਨੈ ਪਤਿ ਸਿਉ ਪਰਗਟੁ ਜਾਇ ॥
ਮੰਨੈ ਮਗੁ ਨ ਚਲੈ ਪੰਥੁ ॥
ਮੰਨੈ ਧਰਮ ਸੇਤੀ ਸਨਬੰਧੁ ॥
ਐਸਾ ਨਾਮੁ ਨਿਰੰਜਨੁ ਹੋਇ ॥
ਜੇ ਕੋ ਮੰਨਿ ਜਾਣੈ ਮਨਿ ਕੋਇ ॥੧੪॥

मंनै मारगि ठाक न पाइ ॥
मंनै पति सिउ परगटु जाइ ॥
मंनै मगु न चलै पंथु ॥
मंनै धरम सेती सनबंधु ॥
ऐसा नामु निरंजनु होइ ॥
जे को मंनि जाणै मनि कोइ ॥१४॥

mannai māragi ṭhāk na pāi ॥
mannai pati siu pargaṭu jāi ॥
mannai maḡu na chalai panthu ॥
mannai dharam setī sanbandhu ॥
aisā nāmu nirañjanu hoi ॥
je ko manni jāṇai mani koi ॥14॥

ਮੰਨੈ ਪਾਵਹਿ ਮੋਖੁ ਦੁਆਰੁ ॥
ਮੰਨੈ ਪਰਵਾਰੈ ਸਾਧਾਰੁ ॥
ਮੰਨੈ ਤਰੈ ਤਾਰੇ ਗੁਰੁ ਸਿਖ ॥
ਮੰਨੈ ਨਾਨਕ ਭਵਹਿ ਨ ਭਿਖ ॥
ਐਸਾ ਨਾਮੁ ਨਿਰੰਜਨੁ ਹੋਇ ॥
ਜੇ ਕੋ ਮੰਨਿ ਜਾਣੈ ਮਨਿ ਕੋਇ ॥੧੫॥

मंनै पावहि मोखु दुआरु ॥
मंनै परवारै साधारु ॥
मंनै तरै तारे गुरु सिख ॥
मंनै नानक भवहि न भिख ॥
ऐसा नामु निरंजनु होइ ॥
जे को मंनि जाणै मनि कोइ ॥१५॥

mannai pāvahi mokhu duāru ॥
mannai parvārai sādhāru ॥
mannai tarai tāre guru sikh ॥
mannai nānak bhavahi na bhikh ॥
aisā nāmu nirañjanu hoi ॥
je ko manni jāṇai mani koi ॥15॥

ਪੰਚ ਪਰਵਾਣ ਪੰਚ ਪਰਧਾਨੁ ॥
ਪੰਚੇ ਪਾਵਹਿ ਦਰਗਹਿ ਮਾਨੁ ॥
ਪੰਚੇ ਸੋਹਹਿ ਦਰਿ ਰਾਜਾਨੁ ॥
ਪੰਚਾ ਕਾ ਗੁਰੁ ਏਕੁ ਧਿਆਨੁ ॥
ਜੇ ਕੋ ਕਹੈ ਕਰੈ ਵੀਚਾਰੁ ॥
ਕਰਤੇ ਕੈ ਕਰਣੈ ਨਾਹੀ ਸੁਮਾਰੁ ॥

पंच परवाण पंच परधानु ॥
पंचे पावहि दरगहि मानु ॥
पंचे सोहहि दरि राजानु ॥
पंचा का गुरु एकु धिआनु ॥
जे को कहै करै वीचारु ॥
करते कै करणै नाही सुमारु ॥

pañch parvāṇ pañch pardhānu ॥
pañche pāvahi dargahi mānu ॥
pañche sohahi dari rājānu ॥
pañchā kā guru eku dhiānu ॥
je ko kahai karai vīchāru ॥
karte kai karṇai nāhī sumāru ॥

ਧੌਲੁ ਧਰਮੁ ਦਇਆ ਕਾ ਪੂਤੁ ॥
ਸੰਤੋਖੁ ਥਾਪਿ ਰਖਿਆ ਜਿਨਿ ਸੂਤਿ ॥
ਜੇ ਕੋ ਬੁਝੈ ਹੋਵੈ ਸਚਿਆਰੁ ॥
ਧਵਲੈ ਉਪਰਿ ਕੇਤਾ ਭਾਰੁ ॥
ਧਰਤੀ ਹੋਰੁ ਪਰੈ ਹੋਰੁ ਹੋਰੁ ॥
ਤਿਸ ਤੇ ਭਾਰੁ ਤਲੈ ਕਵਣੁ ਜੋਰੁ ॥

धौलु धरमु दइआ का पूतु ॥
संतोखु थापि रखिआ जिनि सूति ॥
जे को बुझै होवै सचिआरु ॥
धवलै उपरि केता भारु ॥
धरती होरु परै होरु होरु ॥
तिस ते भारु तलै कवणु जोरु ॥

dhaulu dharmu daiā kā pūtu ॥
santokhu thāpi rakhiā jini sūti ॥
je ko bujhai hovai sachiāru ॥
dhavlai upari ketā bhāru ॥
dharti horu parai horu horu ॥
tis te bhāru talai kavaṇu joru ॥

ਜੀਅ ਜਾਤਿ ਰੰਗਾ ਕੇ ਨਾਵ ॥
ਸਭਨਾ ਲਿਖਿਆ ਵੁੜੀ ਕਲਾਮ ॥
ਏਹੁ ਲੇਖਾ ਲਿਖਿ ਜਾਣੈ ਕੋਇ ॥
ਲੇਖਾ ਲਿਖਿਆ ਕੇਤਾ ਹੋਇ ॥
ਕੇਤਾ ਤਾਣੁ ਸੁਆਲਿਹੁ ਰੂਪੁ ॥
ਕੇਤੀ ਦਾਤਿ ਜਾਣੈ ਕੌਣੁ ਕੂਤੁ ॥

जीअ जाति रंगा के नाव ॥
सभना लिखिआ वुड़ी कलाम ॥
एहु लेखा लिखि जाणै कोइ ॥
लेखा लिखिआ केता होइ ॥
केता ताणु सुआलिहु रूपु ॥
केती दाति जाणै कौणु कूतु ॥

jīa jāti raṅgā ke nāv ॥
sabhnā likhiā vuḍī kalām ॥
ehu lekhā likhi jāṇai koi ॥
lekhā likhiā ketā hoi ॥
ketā tāṇu suālihu rūpu ॥
ketī dāti jāṇai kauṇu kūtu ॥

ਕੀਤਾ ਪਸਾਉ ਏਕੋ ਕਵਾਉ ॥
ਤਿਸ ਤੇ ਹੋਏ ਲਖ ਦਰੀਆਉ ॥
ਕੁਦਰਤਿ ਕਵਣ ਕਹਾ ਵੀਚਾਰੁ ॥
ਵਾਰਿਆ ਨ ਜਾਵਾ ਏਕ ਵਾਰ ॥
ਜੋ ਤੁਧੁ ਭਾਵੈ ਸਾਈ ਭਲੀ ਕਾਰ ॥
ਤੂ ਸਦਾ ਸਲਾਮਤਿ ਨਿਰੰਕਾਰ ॥੧੬॥

कीता पसाउ एको कवाउ ॥
तिस ते होए लख दरीआउ ॥
कुदरति कवण कहा वीचारु ॥
वारिआ न जावा एक वार ॥
जो तुधु भावै साई भली कार ॥
तू सदा सलामति निरंकार ॥१६॥

kītā pasāu eko kavāu ॥
tis te hoe lakh darīāu ॥
kudrati kavaṇ kahā vīchāru ॥
vāriā na jāvā ek vār ॥
jo tudhu bhāvai sāī bhalī kār ॥
tū sadā salāmati niraṅkār ॥16॥

ਅਸੰਖ ਜਪ ਅਸੰਖ ਭਾਉ ॥
ਅਸੰਖ ਪੂਜਾ ਅਸੰਖ ਤਪ ਤਾਉ ॥
ਅਸੰਖ ਗਰੰਥ ਮੁਖਿ ਵੇਦ ਪਾਠ ॥
ਅਸੰਖ ਜੋਗ ਮਨਿ ਰਹਹਿ ਉਦਾਸ ॥
ਅਸੰਖ ਭਗਤ ਗੁਣ ਗਿਆਨ ਵੀਚਾਰ ॥
ਅਸੰਖ ਸਤੀ ਅਸੰਖ ਦਾਤਾਰ ॥

असंख जप असंख भाउ ॥
असंख पूजा असंख तप ताउ ॥
असंख गरंथ मुखि वेद पाठ ॥
असंख जोग मनि रहहि उदास ॥
असंख भगत गुण गिआन वीचार ॥
असंख सती असंख दातार ॥

asaṅkh jap asaṅkh bhāu ॥
asaṅkh pūjā asaṅkh tap tāu ॥
asaṅkh garanth mukhi ved pāṭh ॥
asaṅkh jog mani rahahi udās ॥
asaṅkh bhagat guṇ giān vīchār ॥
asaṅkh satī asaṅkh dātār ॥

ਅਸੰਖ ਸੂਰ ਮੁਹ ਭਖ ਸਾਰ ॥
ਅਸੰਖ ਮੋਨਿ ਲਿਵ ਲਾਇ ਤਾਰ ॥
ਕੁਦਰਤਿ ਕਵਣ ਕਹਾ ਵੀਚਾਰੁ ॥
ਵਾਰਿਆ ਨ ਜਾਵਾ ਏਕ ਵਾਰ ॥
ਜੋ ਤੁਧੁ ਭਾਵੈ ਸਾਈ ਭਲੀ ਕਾਰ ॥
ਤੂ ਸਦਾ ਸਲਾਮਤਿ ਨਿਰੰਕਾਰ ॥੧੭॥

असंख सूर मुह भख सार ॥
असंख मोनि लिव लाइ तार ॥
कुदरति कवण कहा वीचारु ॥
वारिआ न जावा एक वार ॥
जो तुधु भावै साई भली कार ॥
तू सदा सलामति निरंकार ॥१७॥

asaṅkh sūr muh bhakh sār ॥
asaṅkh moni liv lāi tār ॥
kudrati kavaṇ kahā vīchāru ॥
vāriā na jāvā ek vār ॥
jo tudhu bhāvai sāī bhalī kār ॥
tū sadā salāmati niraṅkār ॥17॥

ਅਸੰਖ ਮੂਰਖ ਅੰਧ ਘੋਰ ॥
ਅਸੰਖ ਚੋਰ ਹਰਾਮਖੋਰ ॥
ਅਸੰਖ ਅਮਰ ਕਰਿ ਜਾਹਿ ਜੋਰ ॥
ਅਸੰਖ ਗਲ ਵਢ ਹਤਿਆ ਕਮਾਹਿ ॥
ਅਸੰਖ ਪਾਪੀ ਪਾਪੁ ਕਰਿ ਜਾਹਿ ॥
ਅਸੰਖ ਕੂੜਿਆਰ ਕੂੜੇ ਫਿਰਾਹਿ ॥

असंख मूरख अंध घोर ॥
असंख चोर हरामखोर ॥
असंख अमर करि जाहि जोर ॥
असंख गल वढ हतिआ कमाहि ॥
असंख पापी पापु करि जाहि ॥
असंख कूड़िआर कूड़े फिराहि ॥

asaṅkh mūrakh andh ghor ॥
asaṅkh chor harāmkhor ॥
asaṅkh amar kari jāhi jor ॥
asaṅkh gal vaḍh hatiā kamāhi ॥
asaṅkh pāpī pāpu kari jāhi ॥
asaṅkh kūḍiār kūḍe phirāhi ॥

ਅਸੰਖ ਮਲੇਛ ਮਲੁ ਭਖਿ ਖਾਹਿ ॥
ਅਸੰਖ ਨਿੰਦਕ ਸਿਰਿ ਕਰਹਿ ਭਾਰੁ ॥
ਨਾਨਕੁ ਨੀਚੁ ਕਹੈ ਵੀਚਾਰੁ ॥
ਵਾਰਿਆ ਨ ਜਾਵਾ ਏਕ ਵਾਰ ॥
ਜੋ ਤੁਧੁ ਭਾਵੈ ਸਾਈ ਭਲੀ ਕਾਰ ॥
ਤੂ ਸਦਾ ਸਲਾਮਤਿ ਨਿਰੰਕਾਰ ॥੧੮॥

असंख मलेछ मलु भखि खाहि ॥
असंख निंदक सिरि करहि भारु ॥
नानकु नीचु कहै वीचारु ॥
वारिआ न जावा एक वार ॥
जो तुधु भावै साई भली कार ॥
तू सदा सलामति निरंकार ॥१८॥

asaṅkh malechh malu bhakhi khāhi ॥
asaṅkh nindak siri karahi bhāru ॥
nānaku nīchu kahai vīchāru ॥
vāriā na jāvā ek vār ॥
jo tudhu bhāvai sāī bhalī kār ॥
tū sadā salāmati niraṅkār ॥18॥

ਅਸੰਖ ਨਾਵ ਅਸੰਖ ਥਾਵ ॥
ਅਗੰਮ ਅਗੰਮ ਅਸੰਖ ਲੋਅ ॥
ਅਸੰਖ ਕਹਹਿ ਸਿਰਿ ਭਾਰੁ ਹੋਇ ॥
ਅਖਰੀ ਨਾਮੁ ਅਖਰੀ ਸਾਲਾਹ ॥
ਅਖਰੀ ਗਿਆਨੁ ਗੀਤ ਗੁਣ ਗਾਹ ॥
ਅਖਰੀ ਲਿਖਣੁ ਬੋਲਣੁ ਬਾਣਿ ॥
ਅਖਰਾ ਸਿਰਿ ਸੰਜੋਗੁ ਵਖਾਣਿ ॥
ਜਿਨਿ ਏਹਿ ਲਿਖੇ ਤਿਸੁ ਸਿਰਿ ਨਾਹਿ ॥

असंख नाव असंख थाव ॥
अगम अगम असंख लोअ ॥
असंख कहहि सिरि भारु होइ ॥
अखरी नामु अखरी सालाह ॥
अखरी गिआनु गीत गुण गाह ॥
अखरी लिखणु बोलणु बाणि ॥
अखरा सिरि संजोगु वखाणि ॥
जिनि एहि लिखे तिसु सिरि नाहि ॥

asaṅkh nāv asaṅkh thāv ॥
agam agam asaṅkh loa ॥
asaṅkh kahahi siri bhāru hoi ॥
akhrī nāmu akhrī sālāh ॥
akhrī giānu gīt guṇ gāh ॥
akhrī likhaṇu bolaṇu bāṇi ॥
akhrā siri sañjogu vakhāṇi ॥
jini ehi likhe tisu siri nāhi ॥

ਜਿਵ ਫੁਰਮਾਏ ਤਿਵ ਤਿਵ ਪਾਹਿ ॥
ਜੇਤਾ ਕੀਤਾ ਤੇਤਾ ਨਾਉ ॥
ਵਿਣੁ ਨਾਵੈ ਨਾਹੀ ਕੋ ਥਾਉ ॥
ਕੁਦਰਤਿ ਕਵਣ ਕਹਾ ਵੀਚਾਰੁ ॥
ਵਾਰਿਆ ਨ ਜਾਵਾ ਏਕ ਵਾਰ ॥
ਜੋ ਤੁਧੁ ਭਾਵੈ ਸਾਈ ਭਲੀ ਕਾਰ ॥
ਤੂ ਸਦਾ ਸਲਾਮਤਿ ਨਿਰੰਕਾਰ ॥੧੯॥

जिव फुरमाए तिव तिव पाहि ॥
जेता कीता तेता नाऊ ॥
विणु नावै नाही को थाऊ ॥
कुदरति कवण कहा वीचारु ॥
वारिआ न जावा एक वार ॥
जो तुधु भावै साई भली कार ॥
तू सदा सलामति निरंकार ॥१६॥

jiv phurmāe tiv tiv pāhi ॥
jetā kītā tetā nāū ॥
viṇu nāvai nāhī ko thāū ॥
kudrati kavaṇ kahā vīchārū ॥
vāriā na jāvā ek vār ॥
jo tudhu bhāvai sāī bhalī kār ॥
tū sadā salāmati niraṅkār ॥19॥

ਭਰੀਐ ਹਥੁ ਪੈਰੁ ਤਨੁ ਦੇਹ ॥
ਪਾਣੀ ਧੋਤੈ ਉਤਰਸੁ ਖੇਹ ॥
ਮੂਤ ਪਲੀਤੀ ਕਪੜੁ ਹੋਇ ॥
ਦੇ ਸਾਬੂਣੁ ਲਈਐ ਓਹੁ ਧੋਇ ॥
ਭਰੀਐ ਮਤਿ ਪਾਪਾ ਕੈ ਸੰਗਿ ॥
ਓਹੁ ਧੋਪੈ ਨਾਵੈ ਕੈ ਰੰਗਿ ॥
ਪੁੰਨੀ ਪਾਪੀ ਆਖਣੁ ਨਾਹਿ ॥
ਕਰਿ ਕਰਿ ਕਰਣਾ ਲਿਖਿ ਲੈ ਜਾਹੁ ॥
ਆਪੇ ਬੀਜਿ ਆਪੇ ਹੀ ਖਾਹੁ ॥
ਨਾਨਕ ਹੁਕਮੀ ਆਵਹੁ ਜਾਹੁ ॥੨੦॥

भरीऐ हथु पैरु तनु देह ॥
पाणी धोतै उतरसु खेह ॥
मूत पलीती कपड़ु होइ ॥
दे साबूणु लईऐ ओहु धोइ ॥
भरीऐ मति पापा कै संगि ॥
ओहु धोपै नावै कै रंगि ॥
पुन्नी पापी आखणु नाहि ॥
करि करि करणा लिखि लै जाहु ॥
आपे बीजि आपे ही खाहु ॥
नानक हुकमी आवहु जाहु ॥२०॥

bharīai hathu pairu tanu deh ॥
pāṇī dhotai utrasu kheh ॥
mūt palītī kapaḍu hoi ॥
de sābūṇu laīai ohu dhoi ॥
bharīai mati pāpā kai saṅgi ॥
ohu dhopai nāvai kai raṅgi ॥
punnī pāpī ākhaṇu nāhi ॥
kari kari karṇā likhi lai jāhu ॥
āpe bīji āpe hī khāhu ॥
nānak hukmī āvahu jāhu ॥20॥

ਤੀਰਥੁ ਤਪੁ ਦਇਆ ਦਤੁ ਦਾਨੁ ॥
ਜੇ ਕੋ ਪਾਵੈ ਤਿਲ ਕਾ ਮਾਨੁ ॥
ਸੁਣਿਆ ਮੰਨਿਆ ਮਨਿ ਕੀਤਾ ਭਾਉ ॥
ਅੰਤਰਗਤਿ ਤੀਰਥਿ ਮਲਿ ਨਾਉ ॥
ਸਭਿ ਗੁਣ ਤੇਰੇ ਮੈ ਨਾਹੀ ਕੋਇ ॥
ਵਿਣੁ ਗੁਣ ਕੀਤੇ ਭਗਤਿ ਨ ਹੋਇ ॥
ਸੁਅਸਤਿ ਆਥਿ ਬਾਣੀ ਬਰਮਾਉ ॥
ਸਤਿ ਸੁਹਾਣੁ ਸਦਾ ਮਨਿ ਚਾਉ ॥

तीरथु तपु दइआ दतु दानु ॥
जे को पावै तिल का मानु ॥
सुणिआ मंनिआ मनि कीता भाउ ॥
अंतरगति तीरथि मलि नाउ ॥
सभि गुण तेरे मै नाही कोइ ॥
विणु गुण कीते भगति न होइ ॥
सुअसति आथि बाणी बरमाउ ॥
सति सुहाणु सदा मनि चाउ ॥

tīrathu tapu daiā datu dānu ॥
je ko pāvai til kā mānu ॥
suṇiā manniā mani kītā bhāu ॥
antargati tīrathi mali nāu ॥
sabhi guṇ tere mai nāhī koi ॥
viṇu guṇ kīte bhagati na hoi ॥
suasati āthi bāṇī barmāu ॥
sati suhāṇu sadā mani chāu ॥

ਕਵਣੁ ਸੁ ਵੇਲਾ ਵਖਤੁ ਕਵਣੁ ਕਵਣ ਥਿਤਿ ਕਵਣੁ ਵਾਰੁ ॥
ਕਵਣਿ ਸਿ ਰੁਤੀ ਮਾਹੁ ਕਵਣੁ ਜਿਤੁ ਹੋਆ ਆਕਾਰੁ ॥
ਵੇਲ ਨ ਪਾਈਆ ਪੰਡਤੀ ਜਿ ਹੋਵੈ ਲੇਖੁ ਪੁਰਾਣੁ ॥
ਵਖਤੁ ਨ ਪਾਇਓ ਕਾਦੀਆ ਜਿ ਲਿਖਨਿ ਲੇਖੁ ਕੁਰਾਣੁ ॥
ਥਿਤਿ ਵਾਰੁ ਨਾ ਜੋਗੀ ਜਾਣੈ ਰੁਤਿ ਮਾਹੁ ਨਾ ਕੋਈ ॥
ਜਾ ਕਰਤਾ ਸਿਰਠੀ ਕਉ ਸਾਜੇ ਆਪੇ ਜਾਣੈ ਸੋਈ ॥
ਕਿਵ ਕਰਿ ਆਖਾ ਕਿਵ ਸਾਲਾਹੀ ਕਿਉ ਵਰਨੀ ਕਿਵ ਜਾਣਾ ॥
ਨਾਨਕ ਆਖਣਿ ਸਭੁ ਕੋ ਆਖੈ ਇਕ ਦੂ ਇਕੁ ਸਿਆਣਾ ॥
ਵਡਾ ਸਾਹਿਬੁ ਵਡੀ ਨਾਈ ਕੀਤਾ ਜਾ ਕਾ ਹੋਵੈ ॥
ਨਾਨਕ ਜੇ ਕੋ ਆਪੌ ਜਾਣੈ ਅਗੈ ਗਇਆ ਨ ਸੋਹੈ ॥੨੧॥

कवणु सु वेला वखतु कवणु कवण थिति कवणु वारु ॥
कवणि सि रुती माहु कवणु जितु होआ आकारु ॥
वेल न पाईआ पंडती जि होवै लेखु पुराणु ॥
वखतु न पाइओ कादीआ जि लिखनि लेखु कुराणु ॥
थिति वारु ना जोगी जाणै रुति माहु ना कोई ॥
जा करता सिरठी कउ साजे आपे जाणै सोई ॥
किव करि आखा किव सालाही किउ वरनी किव जाणा ॥
नानक आखणि सभु को आखै इक दू इकु सिआणा ॥
वडा साहिबु वडी नाई कीता जा का होवै ॥
नानक जे को आपौ जाणै अगै गइआ न सोहै ॥२१॥

kavaṇu su velā vakhatu kavaṇu kavaṇ thiti kavaṇu
vāru ॥
kavaṇi si rutī māhu kavaṇu jitu hoā ākāru ॥
vel na pāīā paṇḍatī ji hovai lekhu purāṇu ॥
vakhatu na pāio kādīā ji likhaṇi lekhu kurāṇu ॥
thiti vāru nā jogī jāṇai ruti māhu nā koī ॥
jā kartā sirṭhī kau sāje āpe jāṇai soī ॥
kiv kari ākhā kiv sālāhī kiu varnī kiv jāṇā ॥
nānak ākhaṇi sabhu ko ākhai ik dū iku siāṇā ॥
vaḍā sāhibu vaḍī nāī kītā jā kā hovai ॥
nānak je ko āpau jāṇai agai gaiā na sohai ॥21॥

ਪਾਤਾਲਾ ਪਾਤਾਲ ਲਖ ਆਗਾਸਾ ਆਗਾਸ ॥
ਓੜਕ ਓੜਕ ਭਾਲਿ ਥਕੇ ਵੇਦ ਕਹਨਿ ਇਕ ਵਾਤ ॥
ਸਹਸ ਅਠਾਰਹ ਕਹਨਿ ਕਤੇਬਾ ਅਸੁਲੂ ਇਕੁ ਧਾਤੁ ॥
ਲੇਖਾ ਹੋਇ ਤ ਲਿਖੀਐ ਲੇਖੈ ਹੋਇ ਵਿਣਾਸੁ ॥
ਨਾਨਕ ਵਡਾ ਆਖੀਐ ਆਪੇ ਜਾਣੈ ਆਪੁ ॥੨੨॥

पाताला पाताल लख आगासा आगास ॥
ओड़क ओड़क भालि थके वेद कहनि इक वात ॥
सहस अठारह कहनि कतेबा असुलू इकु धातु ॥
लेखा होइ त लिखीऐ लेखै होइ विणासु ॥
नानक वडा आखीऐ आपे जाणै आपु ॥२२॥

pātālā pātāl lakh āgāsā āgās ॥
oḍak oḍak bhāli thake ved kahani ik vāt ॥
sahas aṭhārah kahani katebā asulū iku dhātu ॥
lekhā hoi ta likhīai lekhai hoi viṇāsu ॥
nānak vaḍā ākhīai āpe jāṇai āpu ॥22॥

ਸਾਲਾਹੀ ਸਾਲਾਹਿ ਏਤੀ ਸੁਰਤਿ ਨ ਪਾਈਆ ॥
ਨਦੀਆ ਅਤੈ ਵਾਹ ਪਵਹਿ ਸਮੁੰਦਿ ਨ ਜਾਣੀਅਹਿ ॥
ਸਮੁੰਦ ਸਾਹ ਸੁਲਤਾਨ ਗਿਰਹਾ ਸੇਤੀ ਮਾਲੁ ਧਨੁ ॥
ਕੀੜੀ ਤੁਲਿ ਨ ਹੋਵਨੀ ਜੇ ਤਿਸੁ ਮਨਹੁ ਨ ਵੀਸਰਹਿ ॥੨੩॥

सालाही सालाहि एती सुरति न पाईआ ॥
नदीआ अतै वाह पवहि समुंदि न जाणीअहि ॥
समुंद साह सुलतान गिरहा सेती मालु धनु ॥
कीड़ी तुलि न होवनी जे तिसु मनहु न वीसरहि ॥२३॥

sālāhī sālāhi etī surati na pāiā ॥
nadīā atai vāh pavahi samundi na jāṇīahi ॥
samunda sāh sultān girhā setī mālu dhanu ॥
kīḍī tuli na hovnī je tisu manhu na vīsrahi ॥23॥

ਅੰਤੁ ਨ ਸਿਫਤੀ ਕਹਣਿ ਨ ਅੰਤੁ ॥
ਅੰਤੁ ਨ ਕਰਣੈ ਦੇਣਿ ਨ ਅੰਤੁ ॥
ਅੰਤੁ ਨ ਵੇਖਣਿ ਸੁਣਣਿ ਨ ਅੰਤੁ ॥
ਅੰਤੁ ਨ ਜਾਪੈ ਕਿਆ ਮਨਿ ਮੰਤੁ ॥
ਅੰਤੁ ਨ ਜਾਪੈ ਕੀਤਾ ਆਕਾਰੁ ॥
ਅੰਤੁ ਨ ਜਾਪੈ ਪਾਰਾਵਾਰੁ ॥
ਅੰਤ ਕਾਰਣਿ ਕੇਤੇ ਬਿਲਲਾਹਿ ॥
ਤਾ ਕੇ ਅੰਤ ਨ ਪਾਏ ਜਾਹਿ ॥

अंतु न सिफती कहणि न अंतु ॥
अंतु न करणै देणि न अंतु ॥
अंतु न वेखणि सुणणि न अंतु ॥
अंतु न जापै किआ मनि मंतु ॥
अंतु न जापै कीता आकारु ॥
अंतु न जापै पारावारु ॥
अंत कारणि केते बिललाहि ॥
ता के अंत न पाए जाहि ॥

antu na siftī kahaṇi na antu ॥
antu na karṇai deṇi na antu ॥
antu na vekhaṇi suṇaṇi na antu ॥
antu na jāpai kiā mani mantu ॥
antu na jāpai kītā ākārū ॥
antu na jāpai pārāvāru ॥
anta kāraṇi kete billāhi ॥
tā ke anta na pāe jāhi ॥

ਏਹੁ ਅੰਤੁ ਨ ਜਾਣੈ ਕੋਇ ॥
ਬਹੁਤਾ ਕਹੀਐ ਬਹੁਤਾ ਹੋਇ ॥
ਵਡਾ ਸਾਹਿਬੁ ਊਚਾ ਥਾਉ ॥
ਊਚੇ ਉਪਰਿ ਊਚਾ ਨਾਉ ॥
ਏਵਡੁ ਊਚਾ ਹੋਵੈ ਕੋਇ ॥
ਤਿਸੁ ਊਚੇ ਕਉ ਜਾਣੈ ਸੋਇ ॥
ਜੇਵਡੁ ਆਪਿ ਜਾਣੈ ਆਪਿ ਆਪਿ ॥
ਨਾਨਕ ਨਦਰੀ ਕਰਮੀ ਦਾਤਿ ॥੨੪॥

ऐहु अंतु न जाणै कोइ ॥
बहुता कहीऐ बहुता होइ ॥
वडा साहिबु ऊचा थाउ ॥
ऊचे उपरि ऊचा नाउ ॥
एवडु ऊचा होवै कोइ ॥
तिसु ऊचे कउ जाणै सोइ ॥
जेवडु आपि जाणै आपि आपि ॥
नानक नदरी करमी दाति ॥२४॥

ehu antu na jāṇai koi ॥
bahutā kahīai bahutā hoi ॥
vaḍā sāhibu ūchā thāu ॥
ūche upari ūchā nāu ॥
evaḍu ūchā hovai koi ॥
tisu ūche kau jāṇai soi ॥
jevaḍu āpi jāṇai āpi āpi ॥
nānak nadarī karamī dāti ॥24॥

ਬਹੁਤਾ ਕਰਮੁ ਲਿਖਿਆ ਨਾ ਜਾਇ ॥
ਵਡਾ ਦਾਤਾ ਤਿਲੁ ਨ ਤਮਾਇ ॥
ਕੇਤੇ ਮੰਗਹਿ ਜੋਧ ਅਪਾਰ ॥
ਕੇਤਿਆ ਗਣਤ ਨਹੀ ਵੀਚਾਰੁ ॥
ਕੇਤੇ ਖਪਿ ਤੁਟਹਿ ਵੇਕਾਰ ॥
ਕੇਤੇ ਲੈ ਲੈ ਮੁਕਰੁ ਪਾਹਿ ॥
ਕੇਤੇ ਮੂਰਖ ਖਾਹੀ ਖਾਹਿ ॥
ਕੇਤਿਆ ਦੂਖ ਭੂਖ ਸਦ ਮਾਰ ॥
ਏਹਿ ਭਿ ਦਾਤਿ ਤੇਰੀ ਦਾਤਾਰ ॥

बहुता करमु लिखिआ ना जाइ ॥
वडा दाता तिलु न तमाइ ॥
केते मंगहि जोध अपार ॥
केतिआ गणत नही वीचारु ॥
केते खपि तुटहि वेकार ॥
केते लै लै मुकरु पाहि ॥
केते मूरख खाही खाहि ॥
केतिआ दूख भूख सद मार ॥
एहि भि दाति तेरी दातार ॥

bahutā karamu likhiā nā jāi ॥
vaḍā dātā tilu na tamāi ॥
kete maṅgahi jodh apār ॥
ketiā gaṇat nahī vīchāru ॥
kete khapi tuṭahi vekār ॥
kete lai lai mukaru pāhi ॥
kete mūrakh khāhī khāhi ॥
ketiā dūkh bhūkh sad mār ॥
ehi bhi dāti terī dātār ॥

ਬੰਦਿ ਖਲਾਸੀ ਭਾਣੈ ਹੋਇ ॥
ਹੋਰੁ ਆਖਿ ਨ ਸਕੈ ਕੋਇ ॥
ਜੇ ਕੋ ਖਾਇਕੁ ਆਖਣਿ ਪਾਇ ॥
ਓਹੁ ਜਾਣੈ ਜੇਤੀਆ ਮੁਹਿ ਖਾਇ ॥
ਆਪੇ ਜਾਣੈ ਆਪੇ ਦੇਇ ॥
ਆਖਹਿ ਸਿ ਭਿ ਕੇਈ ਕੇਇ ॥
ਜਿਸ ਨੋ ਬਖਸੇ ਸਿਫਤਿ ਸਾਲਾਹ ॥
ਨਾਨਕ ਪਾਤਿਸਾਹੀ ਪਾਤਿਸਾਹੁ ॥੨੫॥

बंदि खलासी भाणै होइ ॥
होरु आखि न सकै कोइ ॥
जे को खाइकु आखणि पाइ ॥
ओहु जाणै जेतीआ मुहि खाइ ॥
आपे जाणै आपे देइ ॥
आखहि सि भि केई केइ ॥
जिस नो बखसे सिफति सालाह ॥
नानक पातिसाही पातिसाहु ॥२५॥

bandi khalāsī bhāṇai hoi ॥
horu ākhi na sakai koi ॥
je ko khāiku ākhaṇi pāi ॥
ohu jāṇai jetīā muhi khāi ॥
āpe jāṇai āpe dei ॥
ākhahi si bhi keī kei ॥
jis no bakhse sifti sālāh ॥
nānak pātisāhi pātisāhu ॥25॥

ਅਮੁਲ ਗੁਣ ਅਮੁਲ ਵਾਪਾਰ ॥
ਅਮੁਲ ਵਾਪਾਰੀਏ ਅਮੁਲ ਭੰਡਾਰ ॥
ਅਮੁਲ ਆਵਹਿ ਅਮੁਲ ਲੈ ਜਾਹਿ ॥
ਅਮੁਲ ਭਾਇ ਅਮੁਲਾ ਸਮਾਹਿ ॥
ਅਮੁਲੁ ਧਰਮੁ ਅਮੁਲੁ ਦੀਬਾਣੁ ॥
ਅਮੁਲੁ ਤੁਲੁ ਅਮੁਲੁ ਪਰਵਾਣੁ ॥

अमुल गुण अमुल वापार ॥
अमुल वापारीए अमुल भंडार ॥
अमुल आवहि अमुल लै जाहि ॥
अमुल भाइ अमुला समाहि ॥
अमुलु धरमु अमुलु दीबाणु ॥
अमुलु तुलु अमुलु परवाणु ॥

amul guṇ amul vāpār ॥
amul vāpārīe amul bhaṇḍār ॥
amul āvahi amul lai jāhi ॥
amul bhāi amulā samāhi ॥
amulu dharmu amulu dībāṇu ॥
amulu tulu amulu parvāṇu ॥

ਅਮੁਲੁ ਬਖਸੀਸ ਅਮੁਲੁ ਨੀਸਾਣੁ ॥
ਅਮੁਲੁ ਕਰਮੁ ਅਮੁਲੁ ਫੁਰਮਾਣੁ ॥
ਅਮੁਲੋ ਅਮੁਲੁ ਆਖਿਆ ਨ ਜਾਇ ॥
ਆਖਿ ਆਖਿ ਰਹੇ ਲਿਵ ਲਾਇ ॥
ਆਖਹਿ ਵੇਦ ਪਾਠ ਪੁਰਾਣ ॥
ਆਖਹਿ ਪੜੇ ਕਰਹਿ ਵਖਿਆਣ ॥

अमुलु बखसीस अमुलु नीसाणु ॥
अमुलु करमु अमुलु फुरमाणु ॥
अमुलो अमुलु आखिआ न जाइ ॥
आखि आखि रहे लिव लाइ॥
आखहि वेद पाठ पुराण ॥
आखहि पड़े करहि वखिआण ॥

amulu bakhsīs amulu nīsāṇu ॥
amulu karamu amulu phurmāṇu ॥
amulo amulu ākhiā na jāi ॥
ākhi ākhi rahe liv lāi ॥
ākhahi ved pāṭh purāṇ ॥
ākhahi paḍe karahi vakhiāṇ ॥

ਆਖਹਿ ਬਰਮੇ ਆਖਹਿ ਇੰਦ ॥
ਆਖਹਿ ਗੋਪੀ ਤੈ ਗੋਵਿੰਦ ॥
ਆਖਹਿ ਈਸਰ ਆਖਹਿ ਸਿਧ ॥
ਆਖਹਿ ਕੇਤੇ ਕੀਤੇ ਬੁਧ ॥
ਆਖਹਿ ਦਾਨਵ ਆਖਹਿ ਦੇਵ ॥
ਆਖਹਿ ਸੁਰਿ ਨਰ ਮੁਨਿ ਜਨ ਸੇਵ ॥

आखहि बरमे आखहि इंद ॥
आखहि गोपी तै गोविंद ॥
आखहि ईसर आखहि सिध ॥
आखहि केते कीते बुध ॥
आखहि दानव आखहि देव ॥
आखहि सुरि नर मुनि जन सेव ॥

ākhahi barme ākhahi ind ॥
ākhahi gopī tai govind ॥
ākhahi īsar ākhahi sidh ॥
ākhahi kete kīte budh ॥
ākhahi dānav ākhahi dev ॥
ākhahi suri nar muni jan sev ॥

ਕੇਤੇ ਆਖਹਿ ਆਖਣਿ ਪਾਹਿ ॥
ਕੇਤੇ ਕਹਿ ਕਹਿ ਉਠਿ ਉਠਿ ਜਾਹਿ ॥
ਏਤੇ ਕੀਤੇ ਹੋਰਿ ਕਰੇਹਿ ॥
ਤਾ ਆਖਿ ਨ ਸਕਹਿ ਕੇਈ ਕੇਇ ॥
ਜੇਵਡੁ ਭਾਵੈ ਤੇਵਡੁ ਹੋਇ ॥
ਨਾਨਕ ਜਾਣੈ ਸਾਚਾ ਸੋਇ ॥
ਜੇ ਕੋ ਆਖੈ ਬੋਲੁਵਿਗਾੜੁ ॥
ਤਾ ਲਿਖੀਐ ਸਿਰਿ ਗਾਵਾਰਾ ਗਾਵਾਰੁ ॥੨੬॥

केते आखहि आखणि पाहि ॥
केते कहि कहि उठि उठि जाहि ॥
ऐते कीते होरि करेहि ॥
ता आखि न सकहि केई केइ ॥
जेवडु भावै तेवडु होइ ॥
नानक जाणै साचा सोइ ॥
जे को आखै बोलुविगाड़ु ॥
ता लिखीऐ सिरि गावारा गावारु ॥२६॥

kete ākhahi ākhaṇi pāhi ॥
kete kahi kahi uṭhi uṭhi jāhi ॥
ete kīte hori karehi ॥
tā ākhi na sakahi keī kei ॥
jevaḍu bhāvai tevaḍu hoi ॥
nānak jāṇai sāchā soi ॥
je ko ākhai boluvigāḍu ॥
tā likhīai siri gāvārā gāvāru ॥26॥

ਸੋ ਦਰੁ ਕੇਹਾ ਸੋ ਘਰੁ ਕੇਹਾ ਜਿਤੁ ਬਹਿ ਸਰਬ ਸਮਾਲੇ ॥
ਵਾਜੇ ਨਾਦ ਅਨੇਕ ਅਸੰਖਾ ਕੇਤੇ ਵਾਵਣਹਾਰੇ ॥
ਕੇਤੇ ਰਾਗ ਪਰੀ ਸਿਉ ਕਹੀਅਨਿ ਕੇਤੇ ਗਾਵਣਹਾਰੇ ॥
ਗਾਵਹਿ ਤੁਹਨੋ ਪਉਣੁ ਪਾਣੀ ਬੈਸੰਤਰੁ ਗਾਵੈ ਰਾਜਾ ਧਰਮੁ ਦੁਆਰੇ ॥
ਗਾਵਹਿ ਚਿਤੁ ਗੁਪਤੁ ਲਿਖਿ ਜਾਣਹਿ ਲਿਖਿ ਲਿਖਿ ਧਰਮੁ ਵੀਚਾਰੇ ॥
ਗਾਵਹਿ ਈਸਰੁ ਬਰਮਾ ਦੇਵੀ ਸੋਹਨਿ ਸਦਾ ਸਵਾਰੇ ॥

सो दरु केहा सो घरु केहा जितु बहि सरब समाले ॥
वाजे नाद अनेक असंखा केते वावणहारे ॥
केते राग परी सिउ कहीअनि केते गावणहारे ॥
गावहि तुहनो पउणु पाणी बैसंतरु गावै राजा धरमु दुआरे ॥
गावहि चितु गुपतु लिखि जाणहि लिखि लिखि धरमु वीचारे ॥
गावहि ईसरु बरमा देवी सोहनि सदा सवारे ॥

so daru kehā so gharu kehā jitu bahi sarab samāle ॥
vāje nād anek asaṅkhā kete vāvaṇhāre ॥
kete rāg parī siu kahīani kete gāvaṇhāre ॥
gāvahi tuhno pauṇu pāṇī baisantaru gāvai rājā dharmu duāre ॥
gāvahi chitu gupatu likhi jāṇahi likhi likhi dharmu vīchāre ॥
gāvahi īsaru barmā devī sohani sadā savāre ॥

ਗਾਵਹਿ ਇੰਦ ਇਦਾਸਣਿ ਬੈਠੇ ਦੇਵਤਿਆ ਦਰਿ ਨਾਲੇ ॥
ਗਾਵਹਿ ਸਿਧ ਸਮਾਧੀ ਅੰਦਰਿ ਗਾਵਨਿ ਸਾਧ ਵਿਚਾਰੇ ॥
ਗਾਵਨਿ ਜਤੀ ਸਤੀ ਸੰਤੋਖੀ ਗਾਵਹਿ ਵੀਰ ਕਰਾਰੇ ॥
ਗਾਵਨਿ ਪੰਡਿਤ ਪੜਨਿ ਰਖੀਸਰ ਜੁਗੁ ਜੁਗੁ ਵੇਦਾ ਨਾਲੇ ॥
ਗਾਵਹਿ ਮੋਹਣੀਆ ਮਨੁ ਮੋਹਨਿ ਸੁਰਗਾ ਮਛ ਪਇਆਲੇ ॥
ਗਾਵਨਿ ਰਤਨ ਉਪਾਏ ਤੇਰੇ ਅਠਸਠਿ ਤੀਰਥ ਨਾਲੇ ॥

गावहि इंद इंदासणि बैठे देवतिआ दरि नाले ॥
गावहि सिध समाधी अंदरि गावनि साध विचारे ॥
गावनि जती सती संतोखी गावहि वीर करारे ॥
गावनि पंडित पड़नि रखीसर जुगु जुगु वेदा नाले ॥
गावहि मोहणीआ मनु मोहनि सुरगा मछ पइआले ॥
गावनि रतन उपाए तेरे अठसठि तीरथ नाले ॥

gāvahi ind indāsaṇi baiṭhe devatiā dari nāle ॥
gāvahi sidh samādhī andari gāvani sādh vichāre ॥
gāvani jatī satī santokhī gāvahi vīr karāre ॥
gāvani paṇḍit paḍani rakhīsar jugu jugu vedā nāle ॥
gāvahi mohṇīā manu mohni surgā machh paiāle ॥
gāvani ratan upāe tere aṭhsaṭhi tīrath nāle ॥

ਗਾਵਹਿ ਜੋਧ ਮਹਾਬਲ ਸੂਰਾ ਗਾਵਹਿ ਖਾਣੀ ਚਾਰੇ ॥
ਗਾਵਹਿ ਖੰਡ ਮੰਡਲ ਵਰਭੰਡਾ ਕਰਿ ਕਰਿ ਰਖੇ ਧਾਰੇ ॥
ਸੇਈ ਤੁਧੁਨੋ ਗਾਵਹਿ ਜੋ ਤੁਧੁ ਭਾਵਨਿ ਰਤੇ ਤੇਰੇ ਭਗਤ ਰਸਾਲੇ ॥
ਹੋਰਿ ਕੇਤੇ ਗਾਵਨਿ ਸੇ ਮੈ ਚਿਤਿ ਨ ਆਵਨਿ ਨਾਨਕੁ ਕਿਆ ਵੀਚਾਰੇ ॥
ਸੋਈ ਸੋਈ ਸਦਾ ਸਚੁ ਸਾਹਿਬੁ ਸਾਚਾ ਸਾਚੀ ਨਾਈ ॥
ਹੈ ਭੀ ਹੋਸੀ ਜਾਇ ਨ ਜਾਸੀ ਰਚਨਾ ਜਿਨਿ ਰਚਾਈ ॥

गावहि जोध महाबल सूरा गावहि खाणी चारे ॥
गावहि खंड मंडल वरभंडा करि करि रखे धारे ॥
सेई तुधुनो गावहि जो तुधु भावनि रते तेरे भगत रसाले ॥
होरि केते गावनि से मै चिति न आवनि नानकु किआ वीचारे ॥
सोई सोई सदा सचु साहिबु साचा साची नाई ॥
है भी होसी जाइ न जासी रचना जिनि रचाई ॥

gāvahi jodh mahābal sūrā gāvahi khāṇī chāre ॥
gāvahi khaṇḍ maṇḍal varbhaṇḍā kari kari rakhe dhāre ॥
seī tudhuno gāvahi jo tudhu bhāvani rate tere bhagat rasāle ॥
hori kete gāvani se mai chiti na āvani nānaku kiā vīchāre ॥
soī soī sadā sachu sāhibu sāchā sāchī nāī ॥
hai bhī hosī jāi na jāsī rachnā jini rachāī ॥

ਰੰਗੀ ਰੰਗੀ ਭਾਤੀ ਕਰਿ ਕਰਿ ਜਿਨਸੀ ਮਾਇਆ ਜਿਨਿ ਉਪਾਈ ॥
ਕਰਿ ਕਰਿ ਵੇਖੈ ਕੀਤਾ ਆਪਣਾ ਜਿਵ ਤਿਸ ਦੀ ਵਡਿਆਈ ॥
ਜੋ ਤਿਸੁ ਭਾਵੈ ਸੋਈ ਕਰਸੀ ਹੁਕਮੁ ਨ ਕਰਣਾ ਜਾਈ ॥
ਸੋ ਪਾਤਿਸਾਹੁ ਸਾਹਾ ਪਾਤਿਸਾਹਿਬੁ ਨਾਨਕ ਰਹਣੁ ਰਜਾਈ ॥੨੭॥

रंगी रंगी भाती करि करि जिनसी माइआ जिनि उपाई ॥
करि करि वेखै कीता आपणा जिव तिस दी वडिआई ॥
जो तिसु भावै सोई करसी हुकमु न करणा जाई ॥
सो पातिसाहु साहा पातिसाहिबु नानक रहणु रजाई ॥२७॥

raṅgī raṅgī bhātī kari kari jinsī māiā jini upāī ॥
kari kari vekhai kītā āpṇā jiv tis dī vaḍiāī ॥
jo tisu bhāvai soī karsī hukmu na karṇā jāī ॥
so pātisāhu sāhā pātisāhibu nānak rahṇu rajāī ॥27॥

ਮੁੰਦਾ ਸੰਤੋਖੁ ਸਰਮੁ ਪਤੁ ਝੋਲੀ ਧਿਆਨ ਕੀ ਕਰਹਿ ਬਿਭੂਤਿ ॥
ਖਿੰਥਾ ਕਾਲੁ ਕੁਆਰੀ ਕਾਇਆ ਜੁਗਤਿ ਡੰਡਾ ਪਰਤੀਤਿ ॥
ਆਈ ਪੰਥੀ ਸਗਲ ਜਮਾਤੀ ਮਨਿ ਜੀਤੈ ਜਗੁ ਜੀਤੁ ॥
ਆਦੇਸੁ ਤਿਸੈ ਆਦੇਸੁ ॥
ਆਦਿ ਅਨੀਲੁ ਅਨਾਦਿ ਅਨਾਹਤਿ ਜੁਗੁ ਜੁਗੁ ਏਕੋ ਵੇਸੁ ॥੨੮॥

मुंदा संतोखु सरमु पतु झोली धिआन की करहि बिभूति ॥
खिंथा कालु कुआरी काइआ जुगति डंडा परतीति ॥
आई पंथी सगल जमाती मनि जीतै जगु जीतु ॥
आदेसु तिसै आदेसु ॥
आदि अनीलु अनादि अनाहति जुगु जुगु एको वेसु ॥२८॥

mundā santokhu saramu patu jholī dhiān kī karahi bibhūti ॥
khinthā kālu kuārī kāiā jugati ḍaṇḍā paratīti ॥
āī panthī sagal jamātī mani jītai jagu jītu ॥
ādesu tisai ādesu ॥
ādi anīlu anādi anāhati jugu jugu eko vesu ॥28॥

ਭੁਗਤਿ ਗਿਆਨੁ ਦਇਆ ਭੰਡਾਰਣਿ ਘਟਿ ਘਟਿ ਵਾਜਹਿ ਨਾਦ ॥
ਆਪਿ ਨਾਥੁ ਨਾਥੀ ਸਭ ਜਾ ਕੀ ਰਿਧਿ ਸਿਧਿ ਅਵਰਾ ਸਾਦ ॥
ਸੰਜੋਗੁ ਵਿਜੋਗੁ ਦੁਇ ਕਾਰ ਚਲਾਵਹਿ ਲੇਖੇ ਆਵਹਿ ਭਾਗ ॥
ਆਦੇਸੁ ਤਿਸੈ ਆਦੇਸੁ ॥
ਆਦਿ ਅਨੀਲੁ ਅਨਾਦਿ ਅਨਾਹਤਿ ਜੁਗੁ ਜੁਗੁ ਏਕੋ ਵੇਸੁ ॥੨੯॥

भुगति गिआनु दइआ भंडारणि घटि घटि वाजहि नाद ॥
आपि नाथु नाथी सभ जा की रिधि सिधि अवरा साद ॥
संजोगु विजोगु दुइ कार चलावहि लेखे आवहि भाग ॥
आदेसु तिसै आदेसु ॥
आदि अनीलु अनादि अनाहति जुगु जुगु एको वेसु ॥२९॥

bhugati giānu daiā bhaṇḍārạṇi ghaṭi ghaṭi vājahi nād ॥
āpi nāthu nāthī sabh jā kī ridhi sidhi avarā sād ॥
sañjogu vijogu dui kār chalāvahi lekhe āvahi bhāg ॥
ādesu tisai ādesu ॥
ādi anīlu anādi anāhati jugu jugu eko vesu ॥29॥

ਏਕਾ ਮਾਈ ਜੁਗਤਿ ਵਿਆਈ ਤਿਨਿ ਚੇਲੇ ਪਰਵਾਣੁ ॥
ਇਕੁ ਸੰਸਾਰੀ ਇਕੁ ਭੰਡਾਰੀ ਇਕੁ ਲਾਏ ਦੀਬਾਣੁ ॥
ਜਿਵ ਤਿਸੁ ਭਾਵੈ ਤਿਵੈ ਚਲਾਵੈ ਜਿਵ ਹੋਵੈ ਫੁਰਮਾਣੁ ॥
ਓਹੁ ਵੇਖੈ ਓਨਾ ਨਦਰਿ ਨ ਆਵੈ ਬਹੁਤਾ ਏਹੁ ਵਿਡਾਣੁ ॥
ਆਦੇਸੁ ਤਿਸੈ ਆਦੇਸੁ ॥
ਆਦਿ ਅਨੀਲੁ ਅਨਾਦਿ ਅਨਾਹਤਿ ਜੁਗੁ ਜੁਗੁ ਏਕੋ ਵੇਸੁ ॥੩੦॥

एका माई जुगति विआई तिनि चेले परवाणु ॥
इकु संसारी इकु भंडारी इकु लाए दीबाणु ॥
जिव तिसु भावै तिवै चलावै जिव होवै फुरमाणु ॥
ओहु वेखै ओना नदरि न आवै बहुता एहु विडाणु ॥
आदेसु तिसै आदेसु ॥
आदि अनीलु अनादि अनाहति जुगु जुगु एको वेसु ॥३०॥

ekā māī jugati viāī tini chele parvāṇu ॥
iku sansārī iku bhaṇḍārī iku lāe dībāṇu ॥
jiv tisu bhāvai tivai chalāvai jiv hovai phurmāṇu ॥
ohu vekhai onā nadari na āvai bahutā ehu viḍāṇu ॥
ādesu tisai ādesu ॥
ādi anīlu anādi anāhati jugu jugu eko vesu ॥30॥

ਆਸਣੁ ਲੋਇ ਲੋਇ ਭੰਡਾਰ ॥
ਜੋ ਕਿਛੁ ਪਾਇਆ ਸੁ ਏਕਾ ਵਾਰ ॥
ਕਰਿ ਕਰਿ ਵੇਖੈ ਸਿਰਜਣਹਾਰੁ ॥
ਨਾਨਕ ਸਚੇ ਕੀ ਸਾਚੀ ਕਾਰ ॥
ਆਦੇਸੁ ਤਿਸੈ ਆਦੇਸੁ ॥
ਆਦਿ ਅਨੀਲੁ ਅਨਾਦਿ ਅਨਾਹਤਿ ਜੁਗੁ ਜੁਗੁ ਏਕੋ ਵੇਸੁ ॥੩੧॥

आसणु लोइ लोइ भंडार ॥
जो किछु पाइआ सु एका वार ॥
करि करि वेखै सिरजणहारु ॥
नानक सचे की साची कार ॥
आदेसु तिसै आदेसु ॥
आदि अनीलु अनादि अनाहति जुगु जुगु एको वेसु ॥३१॥

āsaṇu loi loi bhaṇḍār ॥
jo kichhu pāiā su ekā vār ॥
kari kari vekhai sirjaṇhāru ॥
nānak sache kī sāchī kār ॥
ādesu tisai ādesu ॥
ādi anīlu anādi anāhati jugu jugu eko vesu ॥31॥

ਇਕ ਦੂ ਜੀਭੌ ਲਖ ਹੋਹਿ ਲਖ ਹੋਵਹਿ ਲਖ ਵੀਸ ॥
ਲਖੁ ਲਖੁ ਗੇੜਾ ਆਖੀਅਹਿ ਏਕੁ ਨਾਮੁ ਜਗਦੀਸ ॥
ਏਤੁ ਰਾਹਿ ਪਤਿ ਪਵੜੀਆ ਚੜੀਐ ਹੋਇ ਇਕੀਸ ॥
ਸੁਣਿ ਗਲਾ ਆਕਾਸ ਕੀ ਕੀਟਾ ਆਈ ਰੀਸ ॥
ਨਾਨਕ ਨਦਰੀ ਪਾਈਐ ਕੂੜੀ ਕੂੜੈ ਠੀਸ ॥੩੨॥

इक दू जीभौ लख होहि लख होवहि लख वीस ॥
लखु लखु गेड़ा आखीअहि एकु नामु जगदीस ॥
एतु राहि पति पवड़ीआ चड़ीऐ होइ इकीस ॥
सुणि गला आकास की कीटा आई रीस ॥
नानक नदरी पाईऐ कूड़ी कूड़ै ठीस ॥३२॥

ik dū jībhau lakh hohi lakh hovahi lakh vīs ॥
lakhu lakhu geḍā ākhīahi eku nāmu jagdīs ॥
etu rāhi pati pavaḍīā chaḍīai hoi ikīs ॥
suṇi galā ākās kī kīṭā āī rīs ॥
nānak nadarī pāīai kūḍī kūḍai ṭhīs ॥32॥

ਆਖਣਿ ਜੋਰੁ ਚੁਪੈ ਨਹ ਜੋਰੁ ॥
ਜੋਰੁ ਨ ਮੰਗਣਿ ਦੇਣਿ ਨ ਜੋਰੁ ॥
ਜੋਰੁ ਨ ਜੀਵਣਿ ਮਰਣਿ ਨਹ ਜੋਰੁ ॥
ਜੋਰੁ ਨ ਰਾਜਿ ਮਾਲਿ ਮਨਿ ਸੋਰੁ ॥
ਜੋਰੁ ਨ ਸੁਰਤੀ ਗਿਆਨਿ ਵੀਚਾਰਿ ॥
ਜੋਰੁ ਨ ਜੁਗਤੀ ਛੁਟੈ ਸੰਸਾਰੁ ॥
ਜਿਸੁ ਹਥਿ ਜੋਰੁ ਕਰਿ ਵੇਖੈ ਸੋਇ ॥
ਨਾਨਕ ਉਤਮੁ ਨੀਚੁ ਨ ਕੋਇ ॥੩੩॥

आखणि जोरु चुपै नह जोरु ॥
जोरु न मंगणि देणि न जोरु ॥
जोरु न जीवणि मरणि नह जोरु ॥
जोरु न राजि मालि मनि सोरु ॥
जोरु न सुरती गिआनि वीचारि ॥
जोरु न जुगती छुटै संसारु ॥
जिसु हथि जोरु करि वेखै सोइ ॥
नानक उतमु नीचु न कोइ ॥३३॥

ākhaṇi joru chupai nah joru ॥
joru na maṅgaṇi deṇi na joru ॥
joru na jīvaṇi maraṇi nah joru ॥
joru na rāji māli mani soru ॥
joru na suratī giāni vīchāri ॥
joru na jugatī chhuṭai sansāru ॥
jisu hathi joru kari vekhai soi ॥
nānak utamu nīchu na koi ॥33॥

ਰਾਤੀ ਰੁਤੀ ਥਿਤੀ ਵਾਰ ॥
ਪਵਣ ਪਾਣੀ ਅਗਨੀ ਪਾਤਾਲ ॥
ਤਿਸੁ ਵਿਚਿ ਧਰਤੀ ਥਾਪਿ ਰਖੀ ਧਰਮਸਾਲ ॥
ਤਿਸੁ ਵਿਚਿ ਜੀਅ ਜੁਗਤਿ ਕੇ ਰੰਗ ॥
ਤਿਨ ਕੇ ਨਾਮ ਅਨੇਕ ਅਨੰਤ ॥

राती रुती थिती वार ॥
पवण पाणी अगनी पाताल ॥
तिसु विचि धरती थापि रखी धरमसाल ॥
तिसु विचि जीअ जुगति के रंग ॥
तिन के नाम अनेक अनंत ॥

rātī rutī thitī vār ॥
pavaṇ pāṇī agani pātāl ॥
tisu vichi dhartī thāpi rakhī dharamsāl ॥
tisu vichi jīa jugati ke raṅg ॥
tin ke nām anek anant ॥

ਕਰਮੀ ਕਰਮੀ ਹੋਇ ਵੀਚਾਰੁ ॥
ਸਚਾ ਆਪਿ ਸਚਾ ਦਰਬਾਰੁ ॥
ਤਿਥੈ ਸੋਹਨਿ ਪੰਚ ਪਰਵਾਣੁ ॥
ਨਦਰੀ ਕਰਮਿ ਪਵੈ ਨੀਸਾਣੁ ॥
ਕਚ ਪਕਾਈ ਓਥੈ ਪਾਇ ॥
ਨਾਨਕ ਗਇਆ ਜਾਪੈ ਜਾਇ ॥੩੪॥

करमी करमी होइ वीचारु ॥
सचा आपि सचा दरबारु ॥
तिथै सोहनि पंच परवाणु ॥
नदरी करमि पवै नीसाणु ॥
कच पकाई ओथै पाइ ॥
नानक गइआ जापै जाइ ॥३४॥

karamī karamī hoi vīchāru ॥
sachā āpi sachā darbāru ॥
tithai sohani pañch parvāṇu ॥
nadarī karami pavai nīsāṇu ॥
kach pakāī othai pāi ॥
nānak gaiā jāpai jāi ॥34॥

ਧਰਮ ਖੰਡ ਕਾ ਏਹੋ ਧਰਮੁ ॥
ਗਿਆਨ ਖੰਡ ਕਾ ਆਖਹੁ ਕਰਮੁ ॥
ਕੇਤੇ ਪਵਣ ਪਾਣੀ ਵੈਸੰਤਰ ਕੇਤੇ ਕਾਨ ਮਹੇਸ ॥
ਕੇਤੇ ਬਰਮੇ ਘਾੜਤਿ ਘੜੀਅਹਿ ਰੂਪ ਰੰਗ ਕੇ ਵੇਸ ॥
ਕੇਤੀਆ ਕਰਮ ਭੂਮੀ ਮੇਰ ਕੇਤੇ ਕੇਤੇ ਧੂ ਉਪਦੇਸ ॥
ਕੇਤੇ ਇੰਦ ਚੰਦ ਸੂਰ ਕੇਤੇ ਕੇਤੇ ਮੰਡਲ ਦੇਸ ॥
ਕੇਤੇ ਸਿਧ ਬੁਧ ਨਾਥ ਕੇਤੇ ਕੇਤੇ ਦੇਵੀ ਵੇਸ ॥
ਕੇਤੇ ਦੇਵ ਦਾਨਵ ਮੁਨਿ ਕੇਤੇ ਕੇਤੇ ਰਤਨ ਸਮੁੰਦ ॥
ਕੇਤੀਆ ਖਾਣੀ ਕੇਤੀਆ ਬਾਣੀ ਕੇਤੇ ਪਾਤ ਨਰਿੰਦ ॥
ਕੇਤੀਆ ਸੁਰਤੀ ਸੇਵਕ ਕੇਤੇ ਨਾਨਕ ਅੰਤੁ ਨ ਅੰਤੁ ॥੩੫॥

धर्म खंड का एहो धरमु ॥
गिआन खंड का आखहु करमु ॥
केते पवण पाणी वैसंतर केते कान महेस ॥
केते बरमे घाड़ति घड़ीअहि रूप रंग के वेस ॥
केतीआ करम भूमी मेर केते केते धू उपदेस ॥
केते इंद चंद सूर केते केते मंडल देस ॥
केते सिध बुध नाथ केते केते देवी वेस ॥
केते देव दानव मुनि केते केते रतन समुंद ॥
केतीआ खाणी केतीआ बाणी केते पात नरिंद ॥
केतीआ सुरती सेवक केते नानक अंतु न अंतु ॥३५॥

dharam khaṇḍ kā eho dharmu ||
giān khaṇḍ kā ākhahu karamu ||
kete pavaṇ pāṇī vaisantar kete kān mahes ||
kete barme ghāḍati ghaḍiahi rūp raṅg ke ves ||
ketiā karam bhūmī mer kete kete dhū upades ||
kete ind chand sūr kete kete maṇḍal des ||
kete sidh budh nāth kete kete devī ves ||
kete dev dānav muni kete kete ratan samunda ||
ketiā khāṇī ketīā bāṇī kete pāt narinda ||
ketiā suratī sevak kete nānak antu na antu ||35||

ਗਿਆਨ ਖੰਡ ਮਹਿ ਗਿਆਨੁ ਪਰਚੰਡੁ ॥
ਤਿਥੈ ਨਾਦ ਬਿਨੋਦ ਕੋਡ ਅਨੰਦੁ ॥
ਸਰਮ ਖੰਡ ਕੀ ਬਾਣੀ ਰੂਪੁ ॥
ਤਿਥੈ ਘਾੜਤਿ ਘੜੀਐ ਬਹੁਤੁ ਅਨੂਪੁ ॥
ਤਾ ਕੀਆ ਗਲਾ ਕਥੀਆ ਨਾ ਜਾਹਿ ॥
ਜੇ ਕੋ ਕਹੈ ਪਿਛੈ ਪਛੁਤਾਇ ॥
ਤਿਥੈ ਘੜੀਐ ਸੁਰਤਿ ਮਤਿ ਮਨਿ ਬੁਧਿ ॥
ਤਿਥੈ ਘੜੀਐ ਸੁਰਾ ਸਿਧਾ ਕੀ ਸੁਧਿ ॥੩੬॥

गिआन खंड महि गिआनु परचंडु ॥
तिथै नाद बिनोद कोड अनंदु ॥
सरम खंड की बाणी रूपु ॥
तिथै घाड़ति घड़ीऐ बहुतु अनूपु ॥
ता कीआ गला कथीआ ना जाहि ॥
जे को कहै पिछै पछुताइ ॥
तिथै घड़ीऐ सुरति मति मनि बुधि ॥
तिथै घड़ीऐ सुरा सिधा की सुधि ॥३६॥

giān khaṇḍ mahi giānu parchaṇḍu ॥
tithai nād binod koḍ anandu ॥
saram khaṇḍ kī bāṇī rūpu ॥
tithai ghāḍati ghaḍiai bahutu anūpu ॥
tā kīā galā kathīā nā jāhi ॥
je ko kahai pichhai pachhutāi ॥
tithai ghaḍiai surati mati mani budhi ॥
tithai ghaḍiai surā sidhā kī sudhi ॥36॥

ਕਰਮ ਖੰਡ ਕੀ ਬਾਣੀ ਜੋਰੁ ॥
ਤਿਥੈ ਹੋਰੁ ਨ ਕੋਈ ਹੋਰੁ ॥
ਤਿਥੈ ਜੋਧ ਮਹਾਬਲ ਸੂਰ ॥
ਤਿਨ ਮਹਿ ਰਾਮੁ ਰਹਿਆ ਭਰਪੂਰ ॥
ਤਿਥੈ ਸੀਤੋ ਸੀਤਾ ਮਹਿਮਾ ਮਾਹਿ ॥
ਤਾ ਕੇ ਰੂਪ ਨ ਕਥਨੇ ਜਾਹਿ ॥
ਨਾ ਓਹਿ ਮਰਹਿ ਨ ਠਾਗੇ ਜਾਹਿ ॥
ਜਿਨ ਕੈ ਰਾਮੁ ਵਸੈ ਮਨ ਮਾਹਿ ॥
ਤਿਥੈ ਭਗਤ ਵਸਹਿ ਕੇ ਲੋਅ ॥

करम खंड की बाणी जोरु ॥
तिथै होरु न कोई होरु ॥
तिथै जोध महाबल सूर ॥
तिन महि रामु रहिआ भरपूर ॥
तिथै सीतो सीता महिमा माहि ॥
ता के रूप न कथने जाहि ॥
ना ओहि मरहि न ठागे जाहि ॥
जिन कै रामु वसै मन माहि ॥
तिथै भगत वसहि के लोअ ॥

karam khaṇḍ kī bāṇī joru ॥
tithai horu na koī horu ॥
tithai jodh mahābal sūr ॥
tin mahi rāmu rahiā bharpūr ॥
tithai sīto sītā mahimā māhi ॥
tā ke rūp na kathane jāhi ॥
nā ohi marahi na ṭhāge jāhi ॥
jin kai rāmu vasai man māhi ॥
tithai bhagat vasahi ke loa ॥

ਕਰਹਿ ਅਨੰਦੁ ਸਚਾ ਮਨਿ ਸੋਇ ॥
ਸਚ ਖੰਡਿ ਵਸੈ ਨਿਰੰਕਾਰੁ ॥
ਕਰਿ ਕਰਿ ਵੇਖੈ ਨਦਰਿ ਨਿਹਾਲ ॥
ਤਿਥੈ ਖੰਡ ਮੰਡਲ ਵਰਭੰਡ ॥
ਜੇ ਕੋ ਕਥੈ ਤ ਅੰਤ ਨ ਅੰਤ ॥
ਤਿਥੈ ਲੋਅ ਲੋਅ ਆਕਾਰ ॥
ਜਿਵ ਜਿਵ ਹੁਕਮੁ ਤਿਵੈ ਤਿਵ ਕਾਰ ॥
ਵੇਖੈ ਵਿਗਸੈ ਕਰਿ ਵੀਚਾਰੁ ॥
ਨਾਨਕ ਕਥਨਾ ਕਰੜਾ ਸਾਰੁ ॥੩੭॥

करहि अनंदु सचा मनि सोइ ॥
सच खंडि वसै निरंकारु ॥
करि करि वेखै नदरि निहाल ॥
तिथै खंड मंडल वरभंड ॥
जे को कथै त अंत न अंत ॥
तिथै लोअ लोअ आकार ॥
जिव जिव हुकमु तिवै तिव कार ॥
वेखै विगसै करि वीचारु ॥
नानक कथना करड़ा सारु ॥३७॥

karahi anandu sachā mani soi ॥
sach khaṇḍi vasai niraṅkāru ॥
kari kari vekhai nadari nihāl ॥
tithai khaṇḍ maṇḍal varbhaṇḍ ॥
je ko kathai ta anta na anta ॥
tithai loa loa ākār ॥
jiv jiv hukmu tivai tiv kār ॥
vekhai vigsai kari vīchāru ॥
nānak kathnā karaḍā sāru ॥37॥

ਜਤੁ ਪਾਹਾਰਾ ਧੀਰਜੁ ਸੁਨਿਆਰੁ ॥
ਅਹਰਣਿ ਮਤਿ ਵੇਦੁ ਹਥੀਆਰੁ ॥
ਭਉ ਖਲਾ ਅਗਨਿ ਤਪ ਤਾਉ ॥
ਭਾਂਡਾ ਭਾਉ ਅੰਮ੍ਰਿਤੁ ਤਿਤੁ ਢਾਲਿ ॥
ਘੜੀਐ ਸਬਦੁ ਸਚੀ ਟਕਸਾਲ ॥
ਜਿਨ ਕਉ ਨਦਰਿ ਕਰਮੁ ਤਿਨ ਕਾਰ ॥
ਨਾਨਕ ਨਦਰੀ ਨਦਰਿ ਨਿਹਾਲ ॥੩੮॥

जतु पाहारा धीरजु सुनिआरु ॥
अहरणि मति वेदु हथीआरु ॥
भउ खला अगनि तप ताउ ॥
भाँडा भाउ अमृतु तितु ढालि ॥
घड़ीऐ सबदु सची टकसाल ॥
जिन कउ नदरि करमु तिन कार ॥
नानक नदरी नदरि निहाल ॥३८॥

jatu pāhārā dhīraju suniāru ॥
ahraṇi mati vedu hathīāru ॥
bhau khalā agani tap tāu ॥
bhāṇḍā bhāu amr̥tu titu ḍhāli ॥
ghaḍīai sabadu sachī ṭaksāl ॥
jin kau nadari karamu tin kār ॥
nānak nadarī nadari nihāl ॥38॥

॥ ਸਲੋਕੁ ॥

ਪਵਣੁ ਗੁਰੂ ਪਾਣੀ ਪਿਤਾ ਮਾਤਾ ਧਰਤਿ ਮਹਤੁ ॥
ਦਿਵਸੁ ਰਾਤਿ ਦੁਇ ਦਾਈ ਦਾਇਆ ਖੇਲੈ ਸਗਲ ਜਗਤੁ ॥
ਚੰਗਿਆਈਆ ਬੁਰਿਆਈਆ ਵਾਚੈ ਧਰਮੁ ਹਦੂਰਿ ॥
ਕਰਮੀ ਆਪੋ ਆਪਣੀ ਕੇ ਨੇੜੈ ਕੇ ਦੂਰਿ ॥
ਜਿਨੀ ਨਾਮੁ ਧਿਆਇਆ ਗਏ ਮਸਕਤਿ ਘਾਲਿ ॥
ਨਾਨਕ ਤੇ ਮੁਖ ਉਜਲੇ ਕੇਤੀ ਛੁਟੀ ਨਾਲਿ ॥੧॥

॥ सलोकु ॥

पवणु गुरू पाणी पिता माता धरति महतु ॥
दिवसु राति दुइ दाई दाइआ खेलै सगल जगतु ॥
चंगिआईआ बुरिआईआ वाचै धरमु हदूरि ॥
करमी आपो आपणी के नेड़ै के दूरि ॥
जिनी नामु धिआइआ गए मसकति घालि ॥
नानक ते मुख उजले केती छुटी नालि ॥१॥

॥ Saloku ॥

pavaṇu gurū pāṇī pitā mātā dharati mahatu ॥
divasu rāti dui dāī dāiā khelai sagal jagatu ॥
chaṅgiāīā buriāīā vāchai dharamu hadūri ॥
karamī āpo āpṇī ke neḍai ke dūri ॥
jinī nāmu dhiāiā gae maskati ghāli ॥
nānak te mukh ujale ketī chhuṭī nāli ॥1॥

Bibliography

Allied Chambers Transliterated Hindi, Hindi–English Dictionary, rpr., New Delhi: Allied Chambers (India), 1995.

Bhave, Vinoba, *Japuji*, Varanasi: Sarva Seva Sangh Prakashan, 13th edn., 2010 (Hindi).

Chahal, Maneshwar S., *Japuji Sahib: Way to God in Sikhism*, Book I, 2nd edn., 2009, New Delhi: Prakash Books India.

Chauhan, G.S., *Sri Guru Nanak Dev's, Japuji*, Delhi: Hemkunt Publishers, 2001.

Duggal, Kartar Singh (comp. and tr.), *The Japuji: Sikh Morning Prayer*, Delhi: U.B.S. Publishers and Distributors, 2000.

Gandhi, M.K., *An Autobiography or Story of My Experiments with Truth*, Ahmedabad: Navajivan Publishing House, 1959.

———, *Prayer*, comp. and ed. C. Kaji, Ahmedabad: Navjeevan, 1977.

Ghai, O.P., *The Japuji*, New Delhi: Sterling Publishers, 1991.

Kaur, Satnam, *Three Basics of Sikh Religious Thought: Faith, Grace and Prayer*, 2nd rev. edn., Delhi: Pragati Publishers, 2004.

Macauliffe, Max Arthur, *The Sikh Religion: Its Gurus, Sacred Writings and Authors*, vols. 1-2, Delhi: S. Chand & Co., 1963 by arrangement with Oxford University Press, Bombay.

Monier-Williams, M., *A Sanskrit–English Dictionary*, Delhi: Motilal Banarsidass, corrected edn., 2002.

Mother Teresa, *Everything Starts from Prayer: A Full Circle Book*, 2nd repr., 2007, Delhi.

Osho, *The True Name*, vol. II, repr., New Delhi: New Age International, 2001.

Randhawa, G.S., *Guru Nanak's Japuji*, Text (trilingual) tr. & Study, 4th edn. (rev.), Amritsar: Guru Nanak Dev University, 1996.

Randhawa, Gurdip Singh and Charanjit Singh (trs.), *Guru Nanak's Japuji*, New Delhi: Navayug Traders, 1970.

Saxena, S.K., *Ever Unto God: Essays on Gandhi and Religion*, New Delhi: Indian Council of Philosophical Research, reissued, 1995.

———, *Studies in the Metaphysics of Bradley*, London: George Allen and Unwin; New York: Humanities Press, 1967.

Shri Guru Granth Sahibji, Standard 1,430 pages, Amritsar: Bhai Jawahar Singh Kirpal Singh and Co.

Singh, Daljeet, *Essentials of Sikhism*, Amritsar: Singh Brothers, 1994.

Singh, Gopal (tr. and annot.), *Sri Guru Granth Sahib*, vol. 1, Delhi: Gurdas Kapur and Sons, 1960.

Singh, Jagir, *Japu Parkash* (*Tika Japuji Sahib*), Delhi: Rabbi Prakashan, 1996 (Punjabi).

Singh, Manmohan, *Sri Guru Granth Sahib* (tr., English and Punjabi), vol. I, Amritsar: Shiromani Gurudwara Prabandhak Committee, 7th edn., 2004.

Singh, Pritam (ed.), *Sikh Concept of the Divine*, 2nd edn., Amritsar: Guru Nanak Dev University, 2002.

Singh, Sahib, *Sri Guru Granth Sahib Darpan*, vol. I, 3rd edn., Jalandhar: Raj Pubishers, 1972.

Singh, Sangat, *Japuji*, rev. edn., New Delhi: Hind Pocket Books, 1987.

Singh, Teja, *The Japuji or Guru Nanak's Meditation*, 8th edn., Amritsar: Khalsa Brothers, 1978.

Singh, Trilochan, Jodh Singh, Kapur Singh, Harkrishan Singh and Khushwant Singh, *Selections from the Sacred Writings of Sikhs*, London: George Allen and Unwin, 1960.

Singh, Veer (Bhai Sahib), *Santhyā Sri Guru Granth Sahib* (Punjabi), vol. I, 5th edn., 2007.

Singh, Veer, *Sri Guru Granth Kosh*, Amritsar: Khalsa Tract Society, 1960 (Punjabi).

Singh, Wazir, *Japuji* (*The Spiritual Message of Guru Nanak*), Delhi:

National Book Shop, 2009.

Swami Rama, *Japuji: Meditation in Sikhism* (tr. and comm.), USA: Himalayan International Institute of Yoga Science and Philosophy, 1984.

Talib, G.S. (tr.), *Sri Guru Granth Sahib*, vol. I, Patiala: Punjabi University, 1984.

———, *Japuji* (*The Immortal Prayer Chant*), Delhi: Munshiram Manoharlal, 1911.

William Wordsworth's poem composed a few miles above "Tintern Abbey" on revisiting the banks of the Wye during a tour, 13 July 1798.